Stories of
Calvary

Compiled by Mary Fairchild & Wendy Hodges

Stories of
Calvary

Follow the journeys
Of everyday people
Who were changed first at the cross
Then through the ministry of
Calvary Chapel St. Petersburg

With Pastor Danny Hodges

WINEPRESS WP PUBLISHING

WinePress Publishing (PO Box 428, Enumclaw, WA 98022) functions only as book publisher. As such, the ultimate design, content, editorial accuracy, and views expressed or implied in this work are those of the author.

Unless otherwise noted, all Scriptures are taken from the *Holy Bible, New International Version*®, *NIV*®. Copyright © 1973, 1978, 1984 by the International Bible Society. Used by permission of Zondervan. All rights reserved.

Scripture quotations marked NLT are taken from the *Holy Bible, New Living Translation*, copyright © 1996. Used by permission of Tyndale House Publishers, Inc., Wheaton, Illinois 60189. All rights reserved.

ISBN 13: 978-1-57921-906-2
ISBN 10: 1-57921-906-3
Library of Congress Catalog Card Number: 2007924883

Contributing Writers

Richelle Braynen

Irene Byers

Dan Clark

Bob D'Amico

Angela Dennison

Brooke Donnelly

Mary Fairchild

Lana Franklin

Ray Franklin

Patricia Hodson

Elizabeth Jacquier

Doug Lardner

Charles W. Lee

Ellyn Novak

Scott Rodriguez

Diane Sosnoski

Glenn Temme

Table of Contents

Acknowledgments ix

Introduction 11

Chapter 1:   *A Hope and a Future*—Angela Dennison 13

Chapter 2:   *Free From the Fear of Death*—Glenn Temme............. 18

Chapter 3:   *From Giver to Receiver*—Irene Byers....................... 25

Chapter 4:   *Seeking Truth~Knowing Him*—Frank and Jill Dehn .. 31

Chapter 5:   *"Yo, Praise God! Amen!"*—Bob D'Amico 39

Chapter 6:   *Just As You Are*—Richelle Braynen 46

Chapter 7:   *Immeasurably More*—Bill and Terry Oliver 49

Chapter 8:   *Something Missing*—Jeff and Melissa Niven 62

Chapter 9:   *Streams in the Wasteland*—Lana Franklin 65

Chapter 10: *No Longer a Slave to Sin*—Ray Franklin 75

Chapter 11: *A Letter From Prison*—Charles W. Lee 83

Chapter 12: *Bearing Fruit~Bringing Hope*—Chris and Heather
             Moeller 87

Chapter 13: *A New Song to Sing*—Dan Clark............................. 97

Chapter 14: *No Longer a Number*—Elizabeth Jacquier and
             Diane Sosnoski 103

Chapter 15: *Delivered from Darkness*—Brooke Donnelly 108

Chapter 16: *Let Man Not Separate*—David and Marianne
             Marcum.. 117

Chapter 17: *My Weed-Free Life*—Doug Lardner........................... 128

Chapter 18: *Filled With a Mission*—Tony and Ellyn Novak 132

Chapter 19: *There is Joy in Pain*—Patricia Hodson...................... 139

Chapter 20: *Victory Through the Grave of Defeat*—Scott
             Rodriguez 147

Glossary   155

Acknowledgments

I have always dreamed of writing a book, so when Pastor Danny Hodges asked me to help pull this project together, I was delighted with the opportunity to learn from this experience. Many people worked with me behind the scenes to bring this labor of love to completion.

I must begin by thanking Wendy Hodges. I honestly could not have accomplished this undertaking without her help. Wendy, who personally knows so many of our contributors and has prayed for them over the years, brought a unique perspective, with insight into how each story fits into the tapestry of Calvary Chapel. She carefully polished each one until they all shimmered with the Holy Spirit's anointing.

Second, I would like to thank Beth Navage, who offered countless hours of skillful editing to bring clarity and flow to each story. We also took advantage of Kim Corry's exquisite attention to detail and her ability to spot a typo from a mile away. Dustin Marr and Brett Creamer lent an artistic hand as the photographers for our project.

I feel an overwhelming sense of gratitude for the staff ladies at Calvary Chapel who prayed me through this venture. They all know what little patience I have for long-term projects. And I thank God for my husband, Bill, who truly models Christ with his unconditional love for me and his unwavering support that hastens me to follow my dreams.

Last, and most important, I thank my Lord, Jesus Christ. I believe I speak for each of our contributors as I dedicate this project as a thank offering back to You, my Savior. May You use it for Your glory!

Mary Fairchild
General Editor

Introduction

Stories of Calvary is a compilation of testimonies, true stories of everyday people who were changed first at the cross of Calvary and then in some way through the ministry of Calvary Chapel St. Petersburg. This book is volume one. It is my vision, Lord willing, to continue to present future volumes as testaments to God's amazing grace and faithfulness in the lives of His people. It is my earnest prayer that the Lord will be glorified through this work and that many more lives will be touched and changed through these stories of Calvary.

It was our intention to let each individual tell his or her own story in his or her own words. This has allowed for different styles and voices and made for some interesting reading. Primarily, we have edited the stories for grammar, punctuation, and clarity only.

You may notice the phrase "get plugged in" popping up often in the testimonies to follow. Getting plugged in is the concept of becoming relational in the body of Christ, something I emphasize quite often in my teaching ministry at Calvary Chapel. Over the years, I've noticed that it's the people who really get plugged in that soar in their walk with the Lord.

As people have become relational in our church body, many new ministries have formed over the years. You will discover that several of these ministries are mentioned in the stories of Calvary. We have provided a glossary at the back of the book to further explain the high-lighted ministries (in bold print) to readers who are not familiar with our church.

Most of the lives represented in this book have changed dramatically, even since the writing of their stories. God has continued to work His incredible transforming power and pour out wonderful blessings in the lives of these contributors. Some have faced trials to further strengthen their faith. Some have gone on to even greater responsibility in ministry. Although these stories are encapsulated into a fixed space in time, God's work in these individuals, and in all of us who follow Him, will continue until we meet Him in eternity.

Because of Him,

Danny Hodges
Senior Pastor
Calvary Chapel St. Petersburg

Chapter 1

A Hope and a Future

ANGELA DENNISON

"For I know the plans I have for you," declares the LORD, "plans to prosper you and not to harm you, plans to give you hope and a future."

—Jeremiah 29:11

When I walked into Calvary Chapel St. Petersburg in 1997, the only hope I was clinging to was my little girl and a few Bible verses. As a new Christian and a single mother, I was hungry to learn more about Jesus, but I felt crushed from the weight of the whispers and comments I'd heard while visiting several other churches in the area.

At Calvary, I felt a sense of comfort I had never felt before, as if the Holy Spirit was telling me gently, "Welcome. This is what the love of Christ is all about." I was blown away by the genuineness of the teaching of the Word. And there were even people with tattoos, just like me!

Pastor Danny prayed with me at the altar after one of the services. He asked the Lord to strengthen me as a single Christian mother and to reveal His will for our lives in Christ. At that moment, I felt my shame wash away as I realized my daughter and I were welcome and that we had finally found a church home. It was just as it says in His Word: "For God, who said, 'Let light shine out of darkness,' made his light shine in our hearts to give us the light of the knowledge of the glory of God in the face of Christ" (2 Corinthians 4:6). This is exactly what Christ did in my life. He pulled me out from the pit of darkness into His light and grace.

I hesitated to write this testimony. My story may come as a surprise to many. However, it's not just my story. It's God's story of my transformed life. It is only by His power that I stand today. My prayer is that if anyone truly struggling to cope with life reads this, he or she will discover that there is a hope, and that His name is Jesus.

> My prayer is that if anyone truly struggling to cope with life reads this, he or she will discover that there is a hope, and that His name is Jesus.

When I was 17, during my last year in high school, my world as I knew it changed. Many factors played a role in causing me to spiral downward. I began to party and use recreational drugs, and I tried various relationships. Naturally, these bad choices resulted in negative consequences. Then there was another factor that I couldn't control—my parents' divorce—and the painful changes that followed for each of us.

It was right at this difficult time that an old boyfriend from school introduced me to cocaine. Thinking I would use it to numb myself from reality, I soon found myself enslaved by the drug. I had chosen a path I couldn't escape. At a critical age for making decisions about my life and my future, I was choosing the wrong road. I had no hope for a future.

I spent most of my senior year in and out of hospitals and rehab centers for anorexia and cocaine abuse. I couldn't relate to anyone my own age, and I felt completely alone. I kept thinking, *Maybe this time I just won't wake up.* But I always did. I just couldn't escape from myself.

When I was 18 years old and in a state of complete brokenness, I cried out to the Lord, "If You are real, and if there really is a God, prove it to me. I do not want to die. I just want to be free." God breathed life into my broken heart that night, and over time, He did just as I had asked. He proved Himself faithful to me. He never left me, even though I continued to look for happiness elsewhere. I began to be freed from the cocaine addiction, and my frail body slowly strengthened.

Shortly after high school, I entered into a relationship with an older man. He seemed to represent everything fun this world had to offer. I started to slip back into my old ways, going to parties and taking part in the nightlife again. Twice I went back into treatment centers while dating this man. When I came out from my final stay in treatment, I was truly ready for the darkness in my mind, the voices and the paranoia, to end—permanently. As the months went by, I was able to refuse the very things that had caused me to backslide. I believe now that this was because of all the prayers from my family and friends.

I started to see more clearly. I awakened to the reality that happiness is not found in this world, in a relationship with a man, or in any of the things I had desperately sought over the years. The relationship that had seemed so fun when it started no longer appealed to me. It was destroying my walk into recovery. We had already begun to separate and go our opposite ways when I found out I was pregnant.

I was torn. I considered having an abortion. After all, I was only 19 and knew nothing about raising a child. I cried until I was drained of tears. I was so disappointed with myself and the choices I had made. Now those choices involved two lives. I asked the Lord to forgive me, and then said, "If You will take care of us, I will have this baby. I will put all of my trust in You and live for You the rest of my life."

God gave me complete peace, and the transformation began. The Lord provided a job for me at a nursery taking care of babies. When the babies napped, I would read my Bible and books on parenting. There were so many new paths I needed to choose, so I prayed every day for the Lord to show me His will.

I didn't have peace from the Lord when my baby's father asked me to marry him. Even though I said yes to the engagement and moved in with him, as time went by I felt the Lord telling me to get out of the boat in the midst of the storm, just as Peter did. God wanted me to trust Him with my life and the life of my child. I called off the engagement towards the end of my pregnancy. When my little girl, Lillian, was just three months old, we moved out to live with my grandmother. When Lillian was six months old, we were both baptized at a local church. I felt that our new life in Christ had begun.

God made a way for us when there was no way in sight. He opened the floodgates and poured out blessings on me and my daughter. Each day when I woke up, I would ask the Lord to mold me and make me into who He wanted me to be. The only thing that mattered to me was sharing His love with anyone who would listen. This included my daughter, whose name means "lily flower, belonging to God." The Lord provided everything we needed, including a safe and happy home of our own and a way for me to go to college. He knew my future husband awaited me there. He also gave me a teaching job where Lillian could attend preschool right alongside me. The road wasn't easy. There were many challenges to overcome, but I chose to stand on the hope I had in Christ and pray for wisdom. I have never looked back.

The Lord put a hunger in my heart for Jesus alone. He gave me a hope and a future greater than I could have ever imagined. It is more than I deserve. Today, though it is hard for me to believe, I am working at the church—the place where I was welcomed and given a second chance. Here at Calvary Chapel, I married Jason, a man who is a protector and a provider for our family. Most importantly, he loves and serves the Lord. A year after we married, we celebrated a new addition to our family, Elijah, and dedicated him to Jesus. We are fortunate that our parents now attend Calvary Chapel and have rededicated their lives to the Lord.

I discovered that Jesus not only loves us but also shows us how to love like He loves and endure through all the disappointments we face in this world. He teaches us how to pray for the people who have hurt us and, even more significantly, to forgive as He forgives us. He never leaves us or forsakes us. He is all faithful, all knowing, and unchanging.

Of these facts, I am a living, breathing testimony. My husband and I and our two children are so thankful to be among the family of God and share in the fellowship here at Calvary Chapel.

Angela Dennison with her husband, Jason

Chapter 2

Free From the Fear of Death

GLENN TEMME

Since the children have flesh and blood, he too shared in their humanity so that by his death he might destroy him who holds the power of death—that is, the devil— and free those who all their lives were held in slavery by their fear of death.

—Hebrews 2:14–15

C alvary Chapel became my one and only church home in June of 1997, shortly after I read an article in the *St. Petersburg Times* that described a "Bible toting" church. The article captured my attention. As an adult, I had never had a church to call home or even attended one on a regular basis, though I did attend church on Christmas for sentimental reasons. Then I came to know the Lord personally in 1996, while reading the book of Romans.

As a new Christian, I felt compelled to worship, to read the Bible, and to pray. One of the most satisfying experiences was reading through the entire New Testament. As I read and prayed, it became more and more clear that Jesus had plans for me. The words, "Let us not neglect our meeting together, *as some people do*" (Hebrews 10:25, NLT, italics mine), kept ringing in my head. In 1997, while visiting old friends who lived out of state, I went to their church on Sunday. It was my first time in a church as a believer. It was a powerful and convincing experience. I knew for sure that when I got back home to Florida, I was going to find a church home.

I initially tried the local Lutheran church. My brother had been baptized as an infant in the Lutheran church, but due to my parents' poor attendance, the leaders of the church had declined their request to baptize me as an infant. Before becoming a Christian, I had always interpreted these events to mean that the Lutheran church had rejected me even as a child, and that was probably God's evaluation of me as well.

During the summer between seventh and eighth grade, I began to hang out with my brother's older friends. They were part of a gang of 20 or more, ranging in age from 16 to 23. I was one of the youngest, at 13. It was the late '60s, and drugs of all kinds were common. By this time, I had already begun smoking cigarettes habitually, so trying marijuana was a small next step. I didn't really like it, but I wanted to be "one of the guys." No one forced me. It was a personal choice made from a desire to fit in. By the end of the summer, I had tried many other forms of getting high, including "orange sunshine" (LSD). Needless to say, early in life I was quickly heading down the wrong road.

I discovered there were some benefits to getting high, such as not being able to think. From my earliest memories, I can recall continually struggling with thoughts of sexual attraction toward my male friends. I found relief from the shame and guilt of these thoughts when I got high. All I wanted was for these desires to go away. But they wouldn't.

In my confusion, I could not understand why I was having this problem and why it wouldn't go away. Why was I struggling with this? What was wrong with me? Then I heard it! A voice said, "You're struggling with these desires because you were born that way. You're a homosexual, and God made you that way. Why else would these desires be so powerful?"

Why would God do that? I thought. *He says it's wrong. Why would He create me into something He hates?* "Don't you remember?" the voice replied. "They wouldn't baptize you, even when you were a little baby. God rejected you from the beginning. Why fight it? You can't beat it. Besides, you're going to hell anyway. You might as well enjoy yourself and be who you were born to be."

So, at the age of 20, I made the biggest mistake of my life. I believed a lie. It was a lie that would send me down a lonely road. To fit in, I wouldn't tell anyone. To cover the pain, I would abuse drugs.

In the summer of 1988, my father passed away suddenly as he lay on the floor taking a nap. I got a phone call telling me the news. That was my signal to kill the pain, which I did—big time—for the next six months.

I was shocked by the suddenness of death, by not knowing where death had taken my father, and by the permanence of our separation. Being left alone shocked me as well. Dad had always been there for me. Even if we were thousands of miles apart, I knew that if I got into trouble, I could rely on him for help. Physically, Dad was a big man, strong and powerful, able to help in any situation. Now, in a single moment, he was gone. Suddenly, I felt completely on my own. This scared me to death.

After six months of heavy drug use, I was ready for a long vacation. In the spring of 1989, I moved down to Florida to live with my mother and brother. The change was good for me. It separated me from the people who had supplied me with drugs, and I didn't attempt to build new drug contacts. My mind began to clear. God was preparing me.

Living with Mom wasn't bad, except for the annoying Christian program she liked to listen to on the car radio. Every time I got in the car, I had to change the station. Sometimes, however, I would catch myself listening. I was surprised when I realized I was beginning to enjoy the music.

One day, my mom gave me a New Testament. It was the *New Living Translation*, and she said it was easy to read. I had previously thought there was only one translation—the one with all the "thou's." I began reading the Bible again, as I had many other times. I started at the beginning of the New Testament with Matthew and continued reading through the Gospels and then on to Acts. Today, I love the book of Acts, but truthfully, at that point in my life, it almost killed me. It seemed dry and had nothing to do with my life. I felt like I was reading Webster's dictionary.

I did make it through the book of Acts, and then I went on to Romans. What a difference right off the bat! As I read, I knew that what I was reading was truth and that it was talking about me. I believed the message I read. It spoke of who I was; it revealed that I had believed a lie; and it said that Jesus Christ was who He claimed to be, God incarnate. It was the first time in my life that I knew God was speaking directly to me.

As an adult, there had been occasions when people, even friends, told me about Christ. Many times in my 20s and 30s I had started to read the Bible, beginning in Genesis and plodding along, sometimes even into Leviticus, only to give up and put it aside. Through the years, I had read the Gospels several times. But it was God's good plan that Paul would write Romans so that I might be saved. And I thank them both. I still remember reading Romans 8:16 for the first time: "For his Holy Spirit speaks to us deep in our hearts and tells us that we are God's children" (NLT). It rang true in my heart. I knew I was His! I was forgiven! I was mysteriously clean, and the fear of death no longer held me in its grip.

In the early part of June 1997, as I mentioned, I returned home from my vacation knowing that I wanted to find a church. I asked Mom if she would like to go to church with me. She had been hinting in her soft and patient way for many months, and now I was ready. Mom had not been to church in decades, but we would often sing the words from *Favorite Song of All* together with the Brooklyn Tabernacle Choir as I drove us around on errands in town. We had driven by the Lutheran church many times, and Mom mentioned how it might be nice to go there some Sunday. I think she was a little surprised when I asked her to go.

Mom was also very excited. However, as I put on my suit and tie early the next Sunday morning, I was disappointed when Mom told me she wasn't feeling up to going. She had been suffering with rheumatoid arthritis for years, and it was acting up. So I went to the Lutheran church alone that week. It was a small congregation, so everyone knew I was a first-timer. The people were very friendly, and quite a few went out of their way to greet me. The service was nice, although it seemed a little scripted. I have to admit I was taken aback when a woman dressed in a robe served communion. I didn't know if she was a pastor, but as a new Christian I assumed it must be all right. When I got home, I gave Mom the good report about the service. We would go together next Sunday if she were able.

My friend from Pennsylvania came to visit the following Friday. This was his first visit to Florida, and we wanted to enjoy a fishing trip early Saturday morning, so we all turned in early Friday night. During the night, I thought I awoke to a distant voice saying, "Glenn." This was followed by a long pause, and then I again heard the voice say, "Glenn." I listened closely, but I heard nothing more. I lay in bed and eventually fell back to sleep. Apparently, no one else had heard the voice; at least no one stirred. So my friend and I awoke early the next morning, drank a quick cup of coffee, and headed out quietly so we wouldn't wake Mom.

It was a beautiful June day—the first day of summer. The fishing was a bit slow, but it was nice just to enjoy the sun, the water, and the beach. Fishing always makes me hungry, so we stayed only as long as our stomachs allowed. We stopped on the way home and got takeout so Mom could have lunch with us. When we got home, my brother, Girvin, and my friend, Victor, washed down the fishing poles and bait net while I took our lunch into the house. I didn't see Mom, so I took her sandwich to her room. *She is napping,* I thought to myself. *I'll surprise her with this sandwich.* As soon as I entered her room, I knew she was gone. "Girvin! Come here! Quick!" But it was too late. Mom had passed away, probably during the night when I thought I had heard a voice.

Once again, death had come suddenly, rudely, and with no apologies, no perceived warnings. There was no time for farewells or to say, "I love you"—only shock.

What happened? I can't believe this! What are we going to do?

Only one thing kept me from repeating the mistakes of my past when my father had passed away: *I knew* my Savior. I knew *who I was* and *where I was going*. I was God's child, and I was going to heaven. I also knew where Mom was going. Furthermore, I understood we would meet together again in heaven. This did not remove my grief; it simply added comfort to my grief. Now I had assurance in my heart that this life was not the end. I turned to God's Word again and reread His promises to me. It reassured me and gave me relief. I had peace in my heart, even in grief.

I quickly realized I was experiencing God's grace toward me as a one-year-old Christian. It was truly a wonderful blessing from God. It showed me that Christ was real and that my faith in Him was genuine. What else could account for two dramatically different responses to two separate, life-changing events of equal proportion? This faith was real and able to weather the storms of life. The storms would still come, but God would keep me through them.

On June 29, 1997, I attended Calvary Chapel St. Petersburg for the first time. As soon as I came in, the rock 'n' roll style of worship, the clear reading of the Word, and the straightforward teaching each confirmed in my heart that I was home. I have grown in my walk with Jesus Christ at Calvary Chapel. I have learned to express my praise and worship. One day, I raised my hands in praise as we sang "Lift Jesus Higher." I saw others kneel and pray, so I began to kneel and pray. I heard the Word of God taught clearly and completely.

> I share these words with passion so that I may reveal the reality of the person of Jesus Christ. Not who *I* say He is, but who *He* says He is.

As Pastor Danny taught from the Gospel of John, I heard God's voice saying to me, "Take off the grave clothes and let him go." I listened and quit smoking cigarettes for the first time in more than 35 years. I began getting plugged in by joining the Wednesday morning prayer group with Pastor Laird. I became part of a **Life Group** and shared my testimony. I volunteered with Pastor Frank Dehn and the **Men of Arms** and was baptized on September 28, 1997. In October of the following year, I went on my first mission trip to Marion, Honduras, one week before Hurricane Mitch devastated the area, taking 10,000 lives. The small church we helped build stood as a shelter in the storm for the people of the village.

There is a reason why I have written these painful, real-life experiences. Although it is not a pleasant practice, I write with purpose. I share these words with passion so that I may reveal the reality of the person of Jesus Christ. Not who *I* say He is, but who *He* says He is.

I now worship the living God with all my heart. He is the Almighty Creator. He is all-powerful and compassionate. I believe He is a God who can and does heal. To date, He has chosen to let some of the scars of my past remain. Thoughts sometimes come to mind, and some temptations from the past still remain, but these cause me to seek Him all the more. I am learning to say as Paul did, "I myself no longer live" (Galatians 2:20, NLT). Rather than being condemned, I am now free to worship my Creator with obedience, responding to His great love.

I see clearly now who I would have become if I had been left to my own way. I also see what would have become of me in eternity without the Lord. Rather than death, I now face a glorious destination. I follow my Savior in a grateful response for all He has done and for the price He paid for me. I am not perfect or without mistakes, but I am determined to continue on, for His sake and mine. I am looking forward to my heavenly homeland and His appearing soon.

Glenn Temme

Chapter 3

From Giver to Receiver

IRENE BYERS

Remembering the words the Lord Jesus himself said:
"It is more blessed to give than to receive."
—Acts 20:35

When my family moved from lush Lancaster County, Pennsylvania, to a back-in-the-sticks location in North Carolina's Appalachian Mountains in April 1951, I became a preacher's kid and a missionary's kid. Church involvement was automatic. We were thrust into many positions that required reaching out to others. Giving was more natural to me than receiving. At Calvary Chapel, I learned to receive.

On September 26, 2002, I was in an extremely serious automobile accident that placed me into the role of receiver. As my daughter, Anna, and I traveled north on the interstate from her Tampa home toward Ocala to hear a Christian comedian, we were hit by a GMC Yukon. The SUV hydroplaned 200 feet from the southbound lane, across the rain-soaked median, meeting my Honda Accord head on. We were hemmed in by other vehicles, with no place to go. Pictures of my car show it resembling a crumpled-up sheet of aluminum foil.

In a matter of minutes, my life was forever changed. The bones in both my upper and lower legs were snapped completely. The bones in my upper right arm and lower left arm were broken. Several ribs were fractured, and my right kneecap was smashed beyond repair. My right lung also collapsed. Anna suffered a broken collarbone, an injury to her knee ligament, and a herniated disc in her neck.

> In a matter of minutes, my life was forever changed.

Anna remembered everything about the accident, which proved difficult for her to bear. I have absolutely no memories of it before, during, or after it happened. While Anna was airlifted to St. Joseph's Hospital in Tampa, I was cut from the car and then airlifted to the same hospital.

All of my fractures, except my ribs, were compound fractures, meaning many of them protruded through my skin. Because of a dark area that appeared in the CT scans, the doctors first conducted exploratory surgery. Praise God, all of my organs proved to be free from damage, except for my lung. After the exploratory surgery, the orthopedic doctors set about the intense task of putting titanium rods and stainless steel plates into the bones of both legs and both arms. During my eight days in ICU, I was taken back into surgery five or six times.

My stay at St. Joseph's lasted 15 days, after which I spent four weeks in a rehabilitation center. When I was transferred to the rehabilitation facility, I was extremely depressed. God heard my groanings and provided me with a loving Christian roommate, Everlena Mann. She seemed to be *ever leanin'* on the Lord for every segment of her days. When I would cry, she would say, "Miss Irene, you pray to God." Yes, this preacher's kid needed to be reminded.

After the accident, our friends at Calvary jumped in to bless us immediately. At the time, we had been a part of Calvary Chapel for six years. We had become involved in a **Life Group** and a **Salt & Light** group, worked the information counter, volunteered in the bookstore, sung in choir, helped with **Angel Tree**, and more.

When my husband, Jim, got home from work that September afternoon, he realized that his cell phone had been turned off all day. When he checked his voice mail, he discovered that a stranger had left a message saying, "Your wife and daughter have been involved in a serious accident on I-75." End of message. Immediately, Jim called Scott Tunkus, our **Salt & Light** group leader, for support. Scott said, "I'll be right over and go with you wherever you need to go."

In the meantime, Jim called the Florida Highway Patrol. As he waited on hold, our home phone rang. When Jim answered it, a person on staff at St. Joseph's told him, "Mr. Byers, you need to get over here as quickly as possible." Just then, Scott arrived at our door. God directed Jim to grab my address book and call our family and friends as Scott drove him to Tampa. All Jim could do was ask for prayer. He still knew nothing about our condition.

Meanwhile, Scott's wife, Diana, began calling people to ask for prayer. Scott stayed all night with Jim during my 12 hours of surgery. Chuck and Angie Wicker, also members of our **Salt & Light** group, came to the hospital and stayed until four in the morning. It's interesting to note that our **Salt & Light** group had started in January, just seven months before my accident in September. Previously, we did not know these dear friends.

Several weeks later, I asked Jim what he had experienced at St. Joseph's the night of my accident. He said, "When I first got there, I was taken to a private room, where I had to wait for someone to come and talk to me. That was very scary. I didn't know if you and Anna were still alive, or what. After what seemed like an eternity, I finally got to see you. You were in a semiconscious state and didn't seem to know me. You kept saying, 'O God, O God, O God,' over and over. It was like you were crying out to God. Actually, I saw Anna first. In spite of the air bag, she had tons of glass in her hair and was pretty miserable because of it."

During this time, we also received support from our **Life Group**. This group met regularly at Ron and Cindy Neidert's home. We had been part of this group since its beginning. Cindy and others in the group went to bat for me as prayer warriors and advocates for my long healing journey ahead.

I remember nothing from the eight days I spent in the ICU. I have been told that Frank and Stacia Hall came to see me a couple of times, even though they were preparing to leave for missions work in Ghana in just three days. Pastor Danny blessed me with his visits and Pastor Vivian encouraged me with his powerful prayers. Jan Gilson, bookstore manager, kept checking in on me. Many others visited to cheer me and encourage Jim.

The big event was my return home on November 7. I was still unable to put any weight on my arms or legs and was taken home by wheelchair transport. Before this could take place, Jim had Stacie Pounds, a physical therapist, come to our house to evaluate what was needed for my safety at home. **Men of Arms** built three ramps and enlarged one bathroom doorway to accommodate my wheelchair.

Jim was very concerned about how he would be able to take care of me and still operate our business, our source of livelihood. Insurance did not give us the help we so desperately needed, so Jim, in his desperation, talked to Cindy Neidert to see if she had any suggestions for help.

Cindy had the perfect solution: the **Women of Heart** ministry, which, thanks to the vision of Vale Stradley and Nicole Schuenke, had just been birthed. The ministry is an organization comprised of women helping women. I was their guinea pig. And what a project I presented for them! The group sent ladies to help me four hours each day: two hours in the morning and two in the afternoon. My arms weren't strong enough to wheel myself anywhere, and I could not walk yet.

What did these ladies do? Everything! They did the laundry and the dishes and gave me back rubs. They helped me on and off the toilet, gave me manicures and pedicures, shampooed my hair, prepared food—and the list goes on. A total of 33 ladies helped me for more than 200 hours, for seven months.

One lady asked me, "How can you let people do all this for you?"

"I don't have a choice," I replied. "I am so blessed by it. I pray for each person before she comes." It was enriching for each of the ladies and me. Now, I'm so honored to be a team leader for **Women of Heart**. It's the least I can do when I think of what all those ladies did for me.

As a preacher's kid, the words of Luke in Acts 20:35 were drilled into me: "It is more blessed to give than to receive." But here I was on the receiving end, and I felt so blessed because of it. I wanted to reword that verse to say, "It is more blessed to receive." *Lord, if You are blessing me this much, how much are these ladies being blessed in doing this for me?*

In August, just before the accident, Jim and I had purchased a 1995 Honda Accord from Betty Neighbarger. Her husband, Allen, had died in an ultralight plane crash just seven months before my accident. They were dear friends and longtime Calvary Chapel attendees. His car was a newer Accord than the one we had, with dual air bags. Allen's car was the one I chose to drive that September day.

After the all-night surgery, the orthopedic surgeon asked Jim, "Was Irene wearing a seat belt?" Jim said that I had been and that I always set the example for wearing it. He then asked, "Were there air bags in the car?" Jim replied that there were. "You should know," Dr. Peters said, "that the air bags saved Irene's life."

I'm overwhelmed by the fact that Allen's death granted me physical life. Even more amazing is the fact that Jesus died that we might have everlasting life. It doesn't make sense to me that Betty is without her soul mate of 30 years, but I'm beginning to realize that God's sovereign love is not so much for me to comprehend as it is for me to accept.

Am I back to normal? No, and I never will be. Do I have pain? Yes, I have pain every day. But I declare Philippians 4:13, "I can do everything through him who gives me strength." I have determined that I will not entertain my pain, for I do not want to get locked into it. I try my best to keep it at bay at all times. Praise God, I'm walking almost three miles each day. At my orthopedic doctor's direction, I'm doing modified yoga three days each week to strengthen my muscles. Sometimes I must pray myself along, yet I feel so deeply blessed.

My spiritual birth did not take place at Calvary, but the 10 years Jim and I have spent here have impacted my spiritual journey. Perhaps the most amazing part for me is that I have such a caring, loving family of Christian sisters and brothers. They were not shy about giving to me during my time of trouble. I believe we must be willing to receive graciously when we are in need. How else will givers be blessed in their giving?

Irene Byers

Chapter 4
Seeking Truth ~ Knowing Him

FRANK AND JILL DEHN
By Mary Fairchild

"Then you will know the truth, and the truth will set you free."

—John 8:32

Frank and Jill met in 1989, at Penrod's Palace, a popular nightclub at the time. "I noticed her sitting at the end of the bar and asked her to dance," Frank says. "So we danced, and then later on that night I asked her for a date."

"He looked like he was rich," Jill says. "I just wanted to find a rich man to take care of me." And so their life together began.

Jill had grown up in poverty in a large family of 14 children—seven boys and seven girls, to be exact. "I didn't get any attention," she says. Living conditions were difficult. During the winter months, she would try to stay warm in the subzero temperatures by sleeping in her clothes, with two of her sisters. Sexual abuse and verbal abuse darken her memories. "So, with that background," Jill says, "I grew up always wanting attention, mostly from men. Then I got wild after I left the house. I dressed totally inappropriately, in miniskirts, always showing flesh, and was very much into the bar scene."

"Jill stood out and got everybody's attention," says Frank. "That is what drew me to her." Frank's childhood was just as painful. "I lost my real dad to divorce when I was six years old," he says. "I have vivid memories of driving away in the station wagon and seeing the police arrest him for physical abuse against my mom." After divorcing Frank's father, his mother began a cycle of marriages and divorces. "I lost count after about the ninth step-dad," Frank says.

Frank's mother had been a drinker. "However, she was in the business world, so financially we stayed pretty well off," he explains. "But the men she married were always bums. We'd spend a month, two months, six months—they weren't long-term relationships. Then we'd have to separate. She would never keep track of them and never ask for child support. So we had to do a lot of starting over again."

> "My sister was very poor, yet there was this joy and this smile on her face at all times … This attracted me and made me wonder how a poor person could be happy. She gave credit for her happiness to Jesus Christ."

Frank and Jill's unstable backgrounds sent both of them in pursuit of wealth and on a path of wild living. When their paths crossed, the attraction was instant. They dated for a while and eventually moved in together. Jill became pregnant, and they had a child, but sadly the baby girl died after only seven days. Jill was devastated.

This experience shocked Frank into thinking about life, especially about the things his sister, a born-again Christian, had shared with him many times. "My sister was very poor, yet there was this joy and this smile on her face at all times," he says. "This attracted me and made me wonder how a poor person could be happy. She gave credit for her happiness to Jesus Christ."

Frank's sister often witnessed to him, yet he was not receptive. "One day, she prayed that I would buy a Bible and seek the truth," he says. At the time, Frank was working as a bartender and living the bar scene. Remembering those corrupt days, he now admits, "I was just a wicked guy. Jill was home carrying our baby, and I was bartending, flirting with women, gambling, drinking, and coming home at two or three o'clock in the morning."

On the night of the Miami Hurricanes vs. Florida State Seminoles football game, Frank stayed out all night partying and drinking. "Somewhere in the wee hours of the morning, I found myself drunk, looking around and realizing I was surrounded by a bunch of weird individuals," he recalls. Frank wondered to himself what he was doing with all of these strange people.

"The next morning, the words of my sister rang in my head," he says. "They began to echo in my ears all of a sudden as they came to life in me. I wanted to find out if the life that I was living was actually all there was. I drew a line right there. I said to myself, *I'm 33 years old. Is this what life is all about?*" That day, Frank decided to buy a Bible and seek the truth.

Meanwhile, Frank's drunkenness was causing Jill to seek after God. "I kept thinking this was not what I wanted my life to be," she says. Jill was reading the Bible as well, but not for herself. She would look for verses about drunkenness and leave the Bible open for Frank to find, hoping it would get his attention and make him stop drinking.

Although Frank and Jill were motivated by different external forces, both began earnestly searching for meaning in life. Not knowing where to start, Frank bought a King James red-letter Bible. "I just started asking, 'Is this book the truth?' I would say it out loud while I was working, while I was driving," he says. Frank read the Bible and continued to ask questions. Although he was talking to God, it wasn't really what he would call "praying."

Frank eventually quit his bartending job and went back into construction. He made deliberate steps toward God in an effort to show that he was earnest and genuine in his search. One of these steps included listening to Christian radio. He figured the next step toward seeking God would be to go to church. His sister, a member of Calvary Chapel Sunrise, Florida, had encouraged him to visit Calvary Chapel St. Petersburg. So on Easter Sunday, Frank and Jill went to the warehouse in Joe's Creek Industrial Park for an outdoor tent revival service.

"We sat toward the back," Frank says. "Pastor Danny's message (forgive me, Danny) was just really boring to me. I was sitting back, looking around, and then all of a sudden Danny said, 'Hey, is there anyone out there seeking the truth?'" These words grabbed Frank's attention, and he sat up in his chair. "That was exactly what I was doing, I was seeking the truth," he says. Pastor Danny continued by leading in prayer while Frank bowed his head and followed in sincere obedience. "I asked the Lord to forgive me, and I even raised my hand to acknowledge it."

Later that afternoon, Frank and Jill went to the beach. When they returned to their car, someone had placed a tiny paperback Bible on the front seat. Inscribed on the front of the Bible were the words, "Assurance of Salvation." Then on Monday, while Frank was out looking for a full-time job, he stopped at a pay phone and found a tract in the booth that read, "Jesus is coming. Are you ready?"

Yet it wasn't until Wednesday night that Frank received inner affirmation from the Holy Spirit that he was truly saved. While driving home from work that evening, Frank said to himself, *I know.* "When I said *I know*, I suddenly knew," says Frank. "I knew the answer to my question. I knew that Jesus Christ was the truth. I wept for about three weeks straight."

Frank's new excitement about a relationship with Jesus was obvious to Jill. She was attending church with Frank and had started to read the Bible again, but this time for herself. She struggled to understand some of the difficult portions of the Old Testament. As Jill wrestled with God, it seemed as though she could only see an angry, judgmental God. "I couldn't see His forgiveness," Jill says. "I would throw my Bible across the room." But she kept seeking. "I couldn't stop reading. I kept thinking, *He's got to be a loving God.*"

One day, Frank told Jill how much God meant to him. He explained that God was more important to him than his relationship with her. He said that he could live without her, but not without God. These words made an impression on Jill. "That's when I knew he was different," she says. Suddenly, Jill no longer wanted to live with Frank. "I felt that it was wrong for us to live together. I didn't want God to be mad at me, because I felt Frank and God had something going on. I did not want to live with him, and I told him so."

So Frank moved in with his longtime friend, Pete Hilton, who also just recently had become a Christian. Frank and Pete decided to host a casual gathering of Christian friends, and they invited Jill. She almost did not go. "I was just afraid of what kind of weird things were going to happen," Jill says.

At one point, the people in the group all sat in a circle and began to share their testimonies. Jill started to panic, not knowing what she would say. One by one they all spoke, mysteriously skipping over Jill, much to her relief. "Everybody shared a certain point in their life, a certain day, a certain time, a certain event when they accepted God and they were changed," she says. "I was either going to have to make up something or be honest. I was sweating, thinking of all these strangers staring at me." As the conversation turned to other subjects, Jill felt relieved, until the leader stopped and asked Jill if she had anything to say. She blurted out, "I don't really know if I'm saved. I don't really have a testimony."

"I felt that it was wrong for us to live together. I didn't want God to be mad at me, because I felt Frank and God had something going on."

Then the leader said, "I believe that God brought us all together here tonight for Jill." As he spoke the words, Jill felt a warm cloud of love and acceptance literally wrapping around her. "I began to cry," she says. "I don't remember anything that he said after that, but I just knew that God loved me and was personally interested in me. My whole life I wanted attention. I wanted love and attention, and I wanted God." That night in her circle of new friends, Jill prayed the sinner's prayer and accepted the One who had accepted her.

"I felt as if I had taken a shower, and everything I had done in the past was washed away," Jill explains. "After the whole thing ended, I was standing at the table and people were telling me what my life was going to be like. I wondered, *Am I a Christian now? Is this what it means to be saved?* I didn't tell anyone what I was thinking. The leader had left already, and as I was thinking, he popped his head back in and said, 'I just want you to know, no matter what anyone else says, you were saved tonight.'"

As further proof that a true change had occurred in Jill's life, she adds, "When I went home that night, for the first time in my life I was not afraid of the dark." The transformation continued. "I immediately threw out all of my miniskirts, all my short shirts, all my music. I had no desire anymore to go to the bars. Everything was totally different. My viewpoint was different."

Now Frank and Jill were both on the same road, following Christ. But this path of obedience would quickly lead them apart. Frank had been married before meeting Jill and also had a child from that marriage. As he sought direction, godly men such as Pastor Vivian Laird and Pastor Danny encouraged him to separate from Jill and seek reconciliation with his ex-wife. Although Frank had no desire to get back together with his ex-wife, he did desire to please God, and so out of obedience he decided to give God an opportunity to restore his marriage. He started spending time with his ex-wife and his daughter by working on some repair projects at their home.

During this time, God graciously provided a solution for Jill. She was being discipled by Kim Handelsman, a member of Calvary Chapel. "God brought Kim because I was such a strong-willed person, and I needed someone very firm," Jill says. "She taught me that a relationship with God was first and that everything else would flow out of that relationship."

Kim also encouraged Jill to separate from Frank. Not only was Jill in a difficult place emotionally, but also she was forced to entirely depend on God to meet her basic needs. "I had no family here, no job, no car, no food, no money, no place to live, and no friends," she says. "I had nothing. I just cried out to God." Then she patiently waited for Him to meet those needs. "God had my sister in Tennessee call and ask me to go up and live with her while she was pregnant with her second child and help her out. God provided a way for me to totally leave the situation."

"It was a miraculous thing," Frank agrees. "God made provision for her. He took her out of the picture while I had this other task He had for me to do." For about three months, Frank spent quite a bit of time with his ex-wife and daughter. Then God made it clear that reconciliation of the marriage was not part of His plan. "One day, my ex-wife asked, 'Frank, what are you doing? What are your intentions?' Then she went on to say, 'In these 14 years, we've both changed. You can be a father to your daughter and friends with me, but I want you to know that I will never get married to you again.'"

Frank was overjoyed at hearing these words, but he did not show it to his ex-wife. Later, he told Pastor Danny and Pastor Vivian about the conversation. They both agreed that God seemed to be revealing a closed door and releasing Frank from this marriage.

Frank didn't waste any time calling Jill to reestablish contact. Soon after, they completed a series of premarital counseling sessions and then were married by Pastor Danny in a small ceremony. They also began attending a discipleship Bible study based on Colossians 2:7. The study met at Calvary Chapel and was led by Tim and Alyece Thompson. Frank and Jill soaked up the teaching as they began to grow in their relationship with the Lord.

As Frank and Jill became grounded in their faith, God burdened them to serve as janitors for the church. They were faithful for many years as volunteers, quietly cleaning behind the scenes, until one day God opened the doors of ministry for Frank. Pastor Danny asked him to join the church staff in 1998, not only to oversee building maintenance and construction projects but also to be ordained as pastor for the men's ministry. If you know Frank Dehn, you are well acquainted with his energy and enthusiasm for God. He might even still be characterized as wild, yet now in a different context. Frank is well known as a warrior for the Lord.

There are many more chapters to Frank and Jill's story. They have been married since 1992 and have had two children together, Jared and Danielle. In 2003, they readily fostered and later adopted Frank's young nephew, Joseph, when his mother's sudden death left him an orphan. Both Frank and Jill have a strong desire to serve the Lord and a burden to make the truth of Jesus Christ known to anyone who might be seeking Him.

Frank and Jill Dehn with children (left to right) Danielle, Jared, and Joseph

Chapter 5
"Yo, Praise God! Amen!"

Bob D'Amico

For you were once darkness, but now you are light in
the Lord. Live as children of light.

—Ephesians 5:8

I grew up in Niagara Falls, New York, in a family of eight, including
my father, mother, and five brothers and sisters. We were a typical
family of that generation. My father worked, and my mother stayed
home to take care of the kids. My dad was very involved with politics,
and from early on he began grooming me to be the same.

During my early school years, I was a popular, straight-A student.
I participated in sports, student government, and the honor society.
However, in high school, my life began to change drastically. I started
drinking before and after school, smoking weed (marijuana), and hanging around other people who were doing the same things. We were all
being influenced by our environment, and Christ was not a part of it.

Over the next 20 years, my life continued to spiral out of control. There were endless trips to jail, continuous periods of probation, and numerous visits to rehabilitation centers, treatment centers, and detoxification units. One of the most devastating things I faced was becoming detached from my daughter because of a failed marriage. When I did see her, I was too drunk to enjoy our time together.

Satan had me right where he wanted me. I didn't know Jesus Christ. It became more and more evident that my lifestyle was taking a toll on me and my circle of friends. Already, five of the seven of us who had grown up and hung out together had died. Joe, Carmen, and Jimbo had committed suicide. Carey had stolen a truck and driven it into a wall doing 80 miles an hour. Korey B had gone home after a night out, fallen asleep, and never awakened. He was only 35.

One day in 1999, my friend Wally and I were sitting around, splitting a half-gallon of vodka, which we did almost every day at the time. Wally was the elder "statesman" of the group. I told him that I would be going into treatment. He said that he wasn't ready yet but that he would see me in the treatment program in a couple of weeks. So I proceeded into treatment. It was my fifth time in rehab, and it was obvious to me that it would probably be my last. At this point, I started to panic. I didn't want to live, but I didn't want to die. I couldn't get sober, and I couldn't get clean.

Two days after I started treatment, another new patient approached me. He told me that he was very sorry. Confused, I asked, "Why?" He told me that Wally had been found dead the day before from a drug overdose. Wally wouldn't be coming into treatment, nor would he ever again enjoy his four-year-old son, Dylan, whom he loved so very much. What hit me so hard that day was that out of seven of my friends, six were now dead, and I was in treatment.

I left treatment and headed for Florida, and it was there that I first encountered God. I was on the beach, and I yelled out to Him with tears in my eyes, "Lord, help me! Please, help me!" I asked God if He had a plan for me, and He told me that He did. He said it would unfold in Florida. I believed Him. Up until that time, I had never encountered God. But now I had seen Him, felt Him, and even heard Him speak to me!

The journey from my head to my heart was starting to take place. Before this, I had always confessed with my mouth that Jesus was Lord, but now I was starting to believe in my heart. I felt I needed to find a church. At the time, I was living at a halfway house in Pinellas Park called Cornerstone. One Saturday afternoon, two guys from Calvary Chapel, Glenn Temme and Teddy Huff, showed up to give someone else a ride to church. I asked them about their church and if I could go with them sometime. The following week, I joined them for my first service at Calvary Chapel.

During the next six months of my walk with Christ, I still wasn't convinced that God was in charge. I continued to run my own show. But God in His grace and mercy was looking out for me. He was surrounding me with Christian brothers who had been there before and who would be there for me. I still wasn't broken as God wanted me to be. I was trying to keep one foot in the old life and one foot in the new. But the Lord wanted me to be sold out to Him!

> I managed to overdose twice in one week. To my amazement, both times I woke up in the hospital, and there was brother Glenn Temme praying for me.

My life continued to be out of control. I managed to overdose twice in one week. To my amazement, both times I woke up in the hospital, and there was brother Glenn Temme praying for me. He didn't criticize or judge me; he just told me that he loved me, that God loved me, and that I shouldn't worry. He said everything would be okay. God was showing His love to me through fellow Christians. The Lord was now changing my environment through His unconditional love.

Several months later, I was off and running again. This time when I woke up, I was in jail, charged with assault. As I sat there with a black eye, suffering from alcohol withdrawal, the guard told me that I had nothing to worry about; I wouldn't be going anywhere for a while. He also told me that someone had come by and dropped off a Bible. Sure enough, when I opened it up, there was a note: "Don't worry. It will be okay. We're praying for you. God loves you. Brother Glenn." There was also a sheet of paper with a morning meditation from the book of Psalms.

A few days later, I was told that I had a visitor. Sure enough, there was another brother from Calvary, John McEntegart, smiling and saying, "Boy, you look terrible!" But then he assured me, "Don't worry. We love you, and we are praying for you."

The next day, when I went to court, my new Christian brothers were there. They stood and vouched for me, even though I had such a bad drinking problem. The judge let me out and dropped all charges. Surely the Lord was in that courtroom, and I didn't even know it. I was living proof that those who deserve love the least need it the most.

Once I was released, John and Glenn began to show me the Christian walk. They also helped me to focus on three areas: people, places, and things. These were areas in which I needed to change. They put me with other people who were staying away from drinking and drugs "one day at a time." They encouraged me to get involved in a **Life Group** and convicted me about things in my life that were not of the Lord. I slowly started to clean up, from the posters on my walls to the beer ads on my T-shirts.

I decided to start cleaning the church every Saturday night after service. This was not just a job for me. It put me in an environment where I could be ministered to by other Christians. I didn't like doing it at first, because it was very uncomfortable. But eventually it became a real joy and blessing in my life. It was a time of talking and praying to God rather than thinking about myself and how bad my situation was. Gradually, my negative thoughts about having no money and no car (because of the DUIs) became less important to me.

Through this new environment, I was developing a personal relationship with the Lord and a sense of accountability. For the first time in my life, I started to apply some of the suggestions I had heard over and over but never put into practice. As I began to pray in the morning and read my Bible, I noticed that God was speaking to me, guiding and directing me through His Word. I clearly saw that the impact I had on my environment was directly proportional to the time I spent in the Word. The Holy Spirit was taking control of my life. I realized that I had stayed clean long enough to allow the Holy Spirit to begin working in me, and now I saw that I could not be full of the Holy Spirit if I was full of anything else!

I continued to get plugged in at church and was there almost every day of the week. I attended all of the corporate worship services. I started attending a Sunday afternoon men's discipleship group and joined a **Life Group**. A fire was starting to burn within me. God was replacing the old self with the new self, as only He can do.

Gradually I was being transformed, just like the Word says: "And we . . . are being transformed into his likeness with ever-increasing glory, which comes from the Lord, who is the Spirit" (2 Corinthians 3:18). Each day I began to ask, "Lord, give me the strength, the courage, and the boldness to seek and follow You." Realizing that on my own I was nothing, I made the commitment to be steadfast in my walk with Christ and become the best witness I could be. I knew the world would be watching and waiting to say, "I told you so," or, "You hypocrite." I was learning that it was good to be a Christian and know it, but that it was better to be a Christian and show it.

Through belief and faith in Jesus Christ, I had been given victory, by God's grace, over drinking, drugs, and cigarettes. Recently, I also received victory over hepatitis B and C, which I had caught while using drugs.

The Lord, as only He can do, turned my biggest weakness into one of my biggest strengths. I was asked by the leadership of Calvary Chapel to help develop a new Christian recovery house called **Calvary House**. The goal of this new ministry was to provide a Christian environment for men overcoming substance abuse, who were willing to be trained as disciples for Christ. Later, Pastor Danny asked me if I would be willing to serve as director of the program and live in the house with the residents. When I said I would, he asked me how much time I would need to get ready. I told him 24 hours, just enough time to pack a bag and turn in the key to my rented room.

In the meantime, God provided a perfect six-bedroom house that had previously been used for a similar residential program. In September 2004, **Calvary House** opened its doors to three residents in its first week of operation. Since that time, I've been amazed to see God miraculously restore the lives of desperate men who were just as hopeless

43

as I was. And I'm even more amazed that He would use somebody like me to help them. That's why I can't help but shout, "Yo, praise God! Amen!" What God has done for me, He can do for others. Through this ministry of **Calvary House**, I've discovered that true happiness comes through serving others.

My continued, intimate relationship with Jesus Christ has led to the restoration of many of the relationships in my life. I've been able to minister to and pray with family members who have been running from God their entire lives. The Lord has mended a broken relationship with my ex-wife. Although we haven't remarried, we are now friends and are able to discuss and plan our daughter's future and consider her best interests.

Last, but not least, I thank God for saving my daughter, Dee Dee. I was blessed beyond belief when I was able to witness Dee Dee give her life to Christ. On Father's Day of 2002, at Calvary Chapel, she asked Jesus into her heart as her personal Savior. All I could say was, "Yo, praise God! Amen!" So it's fitting to end with the following little poem I wrote that sums up the story of my changed life:

Keeping the Faith
Lord, I thank You so much for answering my prayers.
It seems I've been waiting for so many years.
There were many times I wanted to let go
But I kept on running my own show.
So many times I started to pray
But I didn't know what words to say.
So I started praying the best I knew how
And I really feel You have touched me now.
Also I want to thank You for removing my fears
Because it seems like they're gone now that You are near.
One other thing I want You to know
Now that You've touched me, I'll never let You go.
Thank You, Lord Jesus.
One of Your children, Bob

Bob D'Amico

Chapter 6
Just As You Are

RICHELLE BRAYNEN

For he says, "In the time of my favor I heard you, and
in the day of salvation I helped you." I tell you, now is
the time of God's favor, now is the day of salvation.
                                            —2 Corinthians 6:2

After my dad died, I had a really strong feeling that I needed to find a church. I was being drawn. Jesus was using the mourning I felt at the loss of my father to draw me closer to Him. Second Corinthians 7:10 talks about a sorrow from God that can help us turn away from sin and seek salvation. I believe this is what the Lord was doing in my life by giving me a strong urge to find a church.

Right about this time, I was at work one night cleaning tables when I overheard a man in the next booth talking to my coworker, Alex, about Jesus. I started listening. Alex was asking him questions, so I stopped cleaning and began listening more intently. Eventually, Alex got up and went back into the kitchen, but I stayed and listened to the man as he continued to talk to me about Jesus. Then I asked him, "What is your belief? Are you in a religion?"

"No," he said. "I'm a Christian."

"What church do you go to?" I asked. He took out a pencil and paper and drew a map to Calvary Chapel.

The first time I tried to go to the church, I couldn't find it. The next week I tried a second time, but I still couldn't find it! Determined not to turn back home, I called Calvary Chapel and got directions.

As soon as I walked in the door, it felt right. I was overwhelmed at how everything was exactly what I wanted. When I saw all of the instruments onstage, I immediately loved the church. The first song the band played was "Come, Now is the Time to Worship." That is now my favorite song. After service that day, I went home and said to my boyfriend, "I have found it!" Then I brought our daughter to church, and soon, my boyfriend followed.

In April or May of 2002, I attended a service in which Pastor Danny invited people to come forward at the end and say the prayer of salvation. My boyfriend was with me. I started to shake, my heart started pounding, and I got huge butterflies in my stomach. I knew the Lord was calling me. I was scared to take that step forward, but I knew I wanted to. So, in front of my boyfriend, I got up, went forward, and said the prayer. Five or six other people also went forward to pray for salvation that day. A prayer counselor took me aside, gave me a Bible, and took down some information.

> As soon as I walked in the door, it felt right. I was overwhelmed at how everything was exactly what I wanted. When I saw all of the instruments onstage, I immediately loved the church.

As soon as I gave my life to the Lord, there were many changes in me. One of the biggest changes was that I now had a strong desire to honor God and to marry the man that God had put in my life. So we got married, and the Lord has since given us a son. That was my heart's desire, to have a son.

I'm now involved in a **Salt & Light** group. I'm doing my best to spread the love of Jesus, and I invite you to do the same. My prayer is to bring more people to Jesus and give honor to God all the days of my life.

Richelle Braynen

Chapter 7
Immeasurably More

BILL AND TERRY OLIVER
By Mary Fairchild

Now to him who is able to do immeasurably more than
all we ask or imagine, according to his power that is at
work within us, to him be glory in the church and in
Christ Jesus throughout all generations, for ever and
ever! Amen.

—Ephesians 3:20–21

It was love at first sight when Bill and Terry met. Their relationship
came together swiftly. Twenty-five years later, it was almost torn
apart just as quickly. But God had something else planned; something
immeasurably more wonderful than Bill and Terry could imagine for
their lives.

Both Bill and Terry grew up in Connecticut. Terry was born into
an unsaved family. Her parents divorced when she was one year old.
"I never saw my father again, until I graduated high school," she says.
"I lived with my mother, my grandmother, my grandfather, and three

uncles, so there was a lot of extended family influence in my life. My mom married again when I was 10."

Between the ages of 8 and 10, Terry distinctly remembers two families making a strong impression on her. "That was the only time in my life when I had any Christian influence. During that time, both of these families kind of adopted me, because my mom worked nights and slept days. I really was on my own." One of the families took Terry to Sunday School at their Methodist church, and the other often talked with her about the Bible. "That was the only exposure I had to the Lord," says Terry.

Bill was born into a Catholic family. He remembers his Catholic grandmother reading the Bible, even though he was never taught to read it. Although this was his introduction to the Lord, "There was no relationship," he says. "I was forced. I had to go to church with the family. And I went to Catholic school."

Terry moved to California at age 10 when her mom remarried. Many years later, she met Bill on a visit to Connecticut. "I was living in a house with two friends," Bill recalls. "Terry was in Connecticut, making arrangements to go to college in California. One of my roommates knew her and invited her over. I came home, met her, and asked her out. I never believed in love at first sight, but this really was. Something in me said, *This is the girl that I'm going to marry.*"

Bill and Terry started dating in August and were married on New Year's Eve, 1974. Terry says, "I didn't know I could love someone the way I fell in love with this man overnight. It was just an amazing thing that has never changed."

Bill and Terry were married seven years when their first child, Will, was born. By then they had started a business, moved to St. Petersburg, Florida, and were living in the Feather Sound area. They were experiencing what they described as "the high life." "There was a lot of drinking and lots of wild living that owning a business had allowed us to do," Terry says. "But none of it meant anything. When this child came along, it was truly an epiphany. It was a time of serious reflection on the value of a human life. He was born in 1981, and within months we were visiting a community church."

Bill and Terry's baby was the catalyst that would set the process of coming to salvation in motion for both of them. Terry's would happen quickly, but Bill's would take years. In each case, God would do immeasurably more than either of them could ask or imagine.

"It wasn't until we had our first child that I started to want to know more about the Lord and would attend church services at a non-denominational church," says Bill. "Yet I still didn't have a personal relationship with God. I felt a little bad about sinning, but I would go back and do the same thing. It wasn't until 2000 that I started getting more serious, and not until 2003 that I turned my will over to God."

Terry was 29 years old when Will was born. "I had always had an intellectual searching since I started college," she says. "I wanted to know more about the invisible world and the forces of life. I pursued eastern religion studies in school. The intellectual realm was very attractive to me, especially the intellectualizing of the spirit world."

When Terry delivered her first child, she began to seriously ponder questions about life. She also carried a dark and heavy burden that weighed on her conscience. Hardly anyone knew that Terry had undergone seven abortions prior to giving birth to Will. "All of the crying and drinking that went on before I found the Lord was because I didn't think that I deserved to live," she says. "I had the abortions before I was born again. Then when I gave birth to my son, I cried, 'Dear God, what have I done?'"

> "When I went to church looking for answers, I guess I was looking for forgiveness. And I found it."

Through tears of gratitude still mixed with remorse, but mostly in awe of God's loving-kindness, Terry could not tell her story without remembering the unparalleled forgiveness of God in her life. "When I went to church looking for answers, I guess I was looking for forgiveness. And I found it. God let me have two children after I murdered seven," she says.

Although Terry felt irresistibly drawn to church each week, it appeared to her that Bill was only doing what he had learned in childhood—attending out of obligation to his family. "Bill was not magnetized.

I was. But we were attached at the hip. We had this new baby and a renewed relationship between us. We were a family now."

One Sunday, an organization called Pro Athletes for Christ brought in a guest speaker to Bill and Terry's neighborhood church. "This young man described me," Terry says. "He spoke to the whole congregation, but as far as I was concerned, there wasn't another person in the room. He spoke to me."

At that moment, Terry wanted the joy and peace this young man was describing. "And that's when I received Christ," she says. "It was like the floodgates opened. I started attending three Bible studies a week, and Bill was telling me, 'Terry, enough already. This is a little over the top.' I couldn't get enough. All I kept saying was, 'Oh my God, oh my God, where have I been for 29 years? Why didn't anybody tell me this?' And the fire was blazing inside. My spirit was connected with the Lord." Terry tried to share her excitement with Bill, but he didn't understand. "There was absolutely no quenching the fire in me," she says. "Bill was dragged along for the ride for a very long time."

"When we had our first baby," Bill explains, "I remember lying down in the bed one day, and I put him alongside of me. I just looked at this little thing that I loved so much and started thinking, *How much does God love me?* That had a real impact on me. I still wasn't ready to get involved in a church or Bible study, but I wanted my son to go to church to learn. I wanted him to know about Jesus and the right way to live. So I would go for Terry and Will."

But in his heart, Bill wanted the world and everything in the world. "Our business was very successful when we first started out," he says, "so I tasted wealth. I wanted big houses, fancy cars, lots of money, and what the money could buy me—vacations and being a big shot."

"Recognition was very important to Bill," Terry recalls. "He had to live his life in such a manner that everyone knew he was a big shot."

Bill and Terry's affluent church fit their lifestyle perfectly. "It attracted a lot of professional football players and baseball players, so that was good for me," Bill says. "We would throw these huge parties and have 10 of the Tampa Bay Buccaneers and the coaches there. It was very gratifying for me, because I was playing the role of the big shot. I thought I cared about God. When I was alone, I could feel the Lord tugging on me, but I kept saying, 'Not yet, not yet.'"

Soon, Bill liked going to church, but for the wrong reasons. "I bought a Rolls Royce so I could pull up in it. They would let me park right in the front. That's the kind of crazy stuff I did. I was not giving any thanks to the Lord. It was all about me. I thought I was this wizard in business, and I didn't recognize the Lord."

Bill's resistance to God was very painful for Terry. "It went on for many years," she says. "When he rejected the Lord, I felt like he was rejecting me. This man that I had fallen so madly in love with, who was so in love with me, couldn't understand why I was head over heels for the Lord. It made no sense. Why didn't he want the Lord too?"

In 1984, Bill and Terry's second child, Adam, was born. Yet Terry's joy was overshadowed by the realization that she could not share the excitement of her newfound faith with Bill. "He didn't want it, and he made it known that I was overdoing it," she says. "What was really hard was having two sons, and all I wanted was a home that magnified the name of Jesus, not in our words alone, but in our lives. Yet it seemed like it just wasn't meant to happen. That was the real heartbreak."

As time went on, Bill began to drink more and more. "I was just sick of everything. I was tired of hearing about Bible studies and sick and tired of church and raising my children." Bill was also tired from working so hard to maintain his on-top-of-the-world image. "Along the way, I had built up my company to a pretty successful level and then sold it," he says. "But I remained a partner. This partnership was a disaster. I had gotten into bed with the devil. I wound up being fired by this group, because they now had control of the company."

Suddenly no matter what Bill did, his successful life fell apart. He lost a large sum of money, his reputation in business was tarnished, and the bills were mounting. When Bill's business partners began to spread terrible rumors about him, he and Terry literally felt run off from their neighborhood church. "That was my first step toward trying to get close to the Lord," Bill remembers. "I had an open mind and somewhat of an open heart. That was when we first started coming to Calvary Chapel." This was in 1987.

"I was so broken," Terry recalls. "Financially, we were stricken. The Lord was trying to get Bill's attention, and our family was along for the ride. The kids were going to Shorecrest Preparatory School at that time. I saw this little sign tucked outside the building. It said, 'Calvary Chapel.' The church was meeting in the school auditorium."

At first Bill would not attend, so Terry packed up the kids and went without him. The first Sunday she attended Calvary Chapel, she sensed that the church would one day buy their warehouse. "That day I approached Pastor Danny about it," says Terry. "About six months later, he went out to California and visited a church in a warehouse. He came back and said, 'You know, Terry, we might want to revisit that discussion.' Calvary Chapel ended up buying the building our business had vacated, a warehouse in Joe's Creek Industrial Park."

Bill and Terry stayed at Calvary Chapel for more than two years. "Back then, the church did not have many children," she explains. "It was mostly couples and singles." For several reasons, Terry began to feel led to return to their previous church. "I had my two kids, and there wasn't much for them at the time," she says. She was also dealing with a serious health concern and felt drawn back to her friends at the community church. "By now those business partners had long since moved on, and everyone found out that they had lied about us. Bill also wanted to go back to our community church."

Eventually, Bill started a new pharmaceutical company. "It didn't take long before it became successful," he says. "Now I was 'using' the Lord. I was praying and asking Him to lead and guide me, and He did. But somewhere along the line, I went back into the world. I started drinking heavily again. If there was a drug available, I would take the drug. I knew plenty of doctors, so I could get almost anything I wanted."

Terry also began drinking heavily at that time. She recalls, "The Holy Spirit wouldn't let that go on for me. So I got sober. I went to Alcoholics Anonymous, and Bill didn't. He was not a happy camper about any of this."

The wedge between them that had begun with Terry's salvation widened even more when she became sober. Although Bill experienced brief moments of clarity, most of the time he drank until he didn't know who he was. "That went on for at least two years," says Terry.

"Anytime I approached him about what he was doing with his life, he just didn't want to hear any of it. He didn't want me to have anything to do with the people who were helping me to get sober. He only wanted me to have limited involvement with my church. He was so angry with me all the time. Every moment that wasn't occupied with work or taking the kids to soccer, he drank. My not drinking with him only made him angrier. I had betrayed him."

During those two years of intense strife, Terry sought a Christian counselor. "I came to the place where I just couldn't do it anymore," she says. "I would end up joining him in the heap he was in and drink myself to death like he was doing. So I decided to do something else."

One day, Terry explained to Bill that she was going on a weekend retreat. At the end of the retreat, she decided not to return home. "I just could not do it anymore," she says. "I had one son at home. He was a junior in high school, and I left him home. I didn't know where I was going, and I felt uprooting him was worse. The other son was in college. I didn't have anywhere to go. I slept on a friend's couch until I could figure out what to do. I hadn't worked in 15 years, since the time my kids were born. I didn't know what was going to happen to me."

At the beginning of their separation, Bill continued drinking and living a wild life. "I got with an attorney to completely destroy her," he says. "That was the goal. You find the right attorney, and they can make it possible."

Terry had not intended to rush into a divorce. She explains, "When I said that I was not coming home, I didn't mean I was divorcing him. I just meant that I couldn't live like that anymore." But Bill pushed. He told Terry he couldn't live without a woman. He insisted that she go and file for divorce so he could be free to find another woman. Terry said okay, but it was not what she wanted to do.

Terry was angry with God and stopped attending church. Yet little did she know that her prayers were about to be answered. Surprisingly, Bill was finally beginning to succumb to the God-applied pressure of his adverse circumstances. "Actually, I started going to Calvary Chapel again during this separation period," Bill explains. "When life started getting crazy with attorneys, that's when the Lord really began working on me. I was going to nightclubs, seeing women, just acting totally insane. When I wasn't drunk, I would think, *What am I doing with my life?* I kept hearing God say, 'All the things you wanted—a family, a business, and the things you wanted to do—I've done all these things for you.'"

Bill went to church on Wednesday nights and Sundays. "I started reading the Bible," he says. He even met with Pastor Danny, who counseled him to "go home, get on your face, and ask the Lord to lead you."

Even though Terry had stopped attending church, she hadn't given up on the Lord. "I never abandoned the Bible study I was a part of," she explains. "It's an independent Bible study, one that Debbie Friley, a member of Calvary Chapel, had started 10 years ago. I've been attending it since it began. Unbeknownst to me, Debbie and Wendy Hodges [Pastor Danny's wife] were praying for my marriage."

About five months into their separation, Debbie Friley arranged for Terry and Wendy to meet for lunch. "Boy, did she straighten me out in one quick hour," Terry remembers. "She told me, 'Okay, so he's being a jerk. You don't divorce him. He told you to go to a lawyer and you went? He told you to file for a divorce and you did it? Tell him if he wants a divorce, he'll have to file for one himself.'

"What Wendy did was put some fight back into me," Terry says. "I had lost all my fight, and she urged me to go to battle for my marriage. She reminded me that I could not change Bill, but I could ask God to change me. Then she said, 'You do *not* have to go to that lawyer's office and sign those papers. You need to stop by Calvary Chapel's bookstore and buy the book *The Power of a Praying Wife*. Go home and start reading it and start praying, and don't get up until the Lord speaks to you and something changes.' Her counsel was very direct, which worked for me. I'm a very direct person. It was what needed to happen when it needed to happen. I said, 'Okay, let's go, let's do this.' And I went home and got on my knees and started praying for this man."

Now Bill was praying. And Terry was praying. Debbie and Wendy were praying too. They each were asking God to work. And God was listening! He was preparing to do immeasurably more than any of them could ask or imagine.

Bill started going to Alcoholics Anonymous. Before long, he and Terry began to talk. "We started communicating. God was really coming into my life," says Bill. Soon they were not only communicating but also dating! Bill recalls, "We started dating and enjoying one another." It took nine months, but Bill and Terry got back together.

At the time, Bill was feeling a great deal of pressure at work, so he asked Terry if she would be willing to help him. Terry agreed. She says, "That was part of the reconciliation, that I would be supportive of the business and that we would live our life together."

So together they made a commitment to simplify their lives. "No more of the high life," Terry says. "We started selling houses, getting on our knees before the Lord, praying together, eating together. Our whole relationship had fallen apart. There was nothing left of it, and we just had to start over. We stripped away all that other stuff—the beach condo, the house in the mountains, the big house on the hill—and lived in a two-bedroom apartment until 2001. Then we moved forward with our lives."

> " ... that's when I said, 'I am a filthy rag.' All those 50 years I thought I was the greatest. But I realized I was absolutely nothing."

God wasn't finished, though. He still had work to do with Bill. Although Bill had begun to grow in his knowledge of the Lord, he still had not given his will over to the Lord. "Things were going wonderful in our marriage," he says, "but in business I was still ruthless. I was doing things I shouldn't do, but I didn't care. Then things with my business began to collapse. That was the last thing that had to go, and it did, in July of 2003. That's when I totally surrendered my life to the Lord."

The FBI entered Bill and Terry's place of business early one morning and began questioning their employees and confiscating files. "Another company had been making accusations about things I was doing in my business," Bill explains. "This brought in the federal government with a search warrant. They seized records, computers, lots of things. It was a tough day."

Terry felt this event was Bill's call to the altar from God. "It was a huge ordeal," she says. "We had marshals show up at our business with guns drawn. The things that were said about us were really over the top. I was driving to work when my son called me in an absolute frenzy. They had separated everybody and were interrogating employees, asking questions about really bizarre things that just never happened. My son pleaded, 'Mom, what have you done?' He thought we had done something horrific. Anyone would have thought so, until the interrogators started getting all the same answers to all the same questions. I knew the Lord was doing what He had to do in Bill's life, and it was very painful. It was not what I would have wanted, but the Lord is my Lord, and He's Bill's Lord too. He did what He had to do. I just had to trust Him."

When Terry's son reached her on the phone that morning, she was driving right by Calvary Chapel. "I looped back and stopped by the church to ask if someone could please go and help my husband," she says. "One of the associate pastors, Jim O'Connor, got in his car and drove to our office. That day, I came running to Calvary Chapel, to this fellowship where God's people could minister to us, which is something Calvary does so beautifully. The Lord has flooded the church with people who minister to others by the Lord's power. In 1987, when Bill wanted no part of the conviction of the Holy Spirit, he couldn't stand being in Calvary Chapel. The presence of the Holy Spirit was too convicting, and he ran from it. We were drawn back to this place after the Lord had prepared Bill to be ministered to."

Nothing ever came of the federal investigation into their business. "They seized all of our records, and they still have them," says Terry. "But the Feds have just ignored it ever since." That day, however, God used this crisis to finally get Bill's attention. "This is what brought Bill to the point of submitting his entire life—and business—completely to the Lord," says Terry.

Indeed, that summer day in 2003 marked the turning point for Bill. "I was sitting outside the office at a picnic bench, and that's when I said, 'I am just a filthy rag.' All those 50 some years I thought I was the greatest. But I realized I was absolutely nothing. And I decided whatever time I had left, I would pray for my sons and hope that they would see the difference in me. Now I'm on my knees, I read God's Word, and I get involved in ministry. The Lord is my everything now. Our business belongs to Him too."

Bill began to see God's amazing power operating in his life. "No matter what's happened in the past three years, nothing has taken my eyes off the Lord. I'm just amazed at what He can do. When I see the things He does, when I experience it, I just say, 'Wow!' And I didn't do anything. I'm just here. I'm not good at attending AA [Alcoholics Anonymous] meetings, but God is taking that desire to drink totally away from me. Being in business, I travel a lot, and there are plenty of opportunities to drink. While I could easily do it, I have zero desire to drink! I'm still kind of tough on the kids, but I'm hoping it's in a loving way. God definitely made this change. Now I don't have to be the big shot, nor do I desire to be that way anymore."

"Our marriage is transformed," says Terry. "Bill used to be so angry and so resentful about my active involvement in AA, and now he's not. Only God could remove that kind of anger and resentment." Terry feels her mission field now is to bring the message of the hope of eternal life in Jesus Christ to women in Alcoholics Anonymous. She has had the privilege of leading others to Christ who sponsored her over the years, as well as those whom she has sponsored. "It's not a formal ministry, but it's the living out of my faith in my life," she says. "There's no question in my mind that the Lord has plopped me smack-dab in the middle of AA to bring people to Him and to bring people back to Him."

Recently, Bill found unexpected joy, adventure, and brotherly friendship when he participated in a disaster-relief effort sent out from Calvary Chapel to help rebuild after Hurricane Katrina. Terry says, "I'm so glad he was willing to go on that trip, because it impacted his life dramatically, as mission trips always do."

Bill says, "There were 13 of us that went, and I'll tell you what. I wouldn't want to face those 13 guys alone, but they were the gentlest, kindest fellows that I've ever been with in my life. We got along so well and cared for one another. Years ago, guys in the church were not the kind of people I wanted to hang around with. But I found that while Pastor Frank [Dehn] is possibly the craziest fellow I know, he's also just a God-loving individual. And he's so much fun. All the guys on the team were tough guys. Yet it was amazing how we could all get down on our knees to pray, hold hands, and give all the glory to Jesus. It impacted my life. We gutted several houses. We were exhausted, yet still had the energy to keep going. It was quite an experience. I'm really looking forward to going on my next mission trip to Guatemala. Now I'm learning to obey the Lord."

Bill has learned another valuable lesson from his brothers at Calvary Chapel. "For men, the world expects so much from us," he says. "With our lives, our wives, our children, we're supposed to be these real macho guys. At least that is what I believed. Now I've found that not to be true. The Lord is gentle and loving, yet powerful, and He commands us to be kind and loving too. I was never good at this before. I find it's such a nicer life to be gentle, kind, and loving. And I think that makes me pretty macho."

Throughout long years of waiting for God to begin his work in Bill's life, Terry learned not to give up the good fight of faith. "During those years I was very depressed," she says. "I took medication for depression, but it didn't work. I was just absolutely broken and had no strength to fight. I think things could have been different if I had not lost that fight. But Wendy brought me the message. Fight! That day the Lord used her feistiness, and I was energized in a way I had not been in years. It was the key that enabled me to continue to go on. All kinds of awesome things happened as a result."

God had one more amazing gift for Terry—a secret desire of her heart He wanted to fulfill. Terry had been baptized by Pastor Danny in 1989, during the sunrise service on Easter Sunday. "It was the desire of my heart to see Bill get baptized," she says. "So every year I would give him the elbow, until finally the elbow quit, and I just let it go. Then it became the hidden secret of my heart. Nobody knew but me and the Lord."

In 2005, Bill and Terry went on a trip to Israel with Calvary Chapel. Bill decided he wanted to be baptized in the Jordan River. He said, "If I'm going to get baptized, I'm going to do it right where Jesus did." Terry says, "It was especially significant to me, because it was during those last five years of our marriage, when we experienced one renewal after another. Our dead marriage was raised to life, one incident at a time, and that baptism was part of it." Bill and Terry were baptized together. Bill recalls, "The interesting thing is she didn't know I was planning to get baptized then. When Pastor Danny asked who wanted to be baptized, she had no idea. She was so surprised!"

This New Year's Eve, Bill and Terry celebrated 32 years of marriage. Their relationship, that began with love at first sight, has endured the test of time and severe trials. They have watched the powerful and faithful hand of God working in their lives to accomplish immeasurably more than either of them could ever imagine. To Him they give glory in the church and in Jesus Christ, forever and ever!

Bill and Terry Oliver

Chapter 8

Something Missing

JEFF AND MELISSA NIVEN
By Mary Fairchild

Why spend money on what is not bread, and your labor on what does not satisfy? Listen, listen to me, and eat what is good, and your soul will delight in the richest of fare.

—Isaiah 55:2

After 10 years of marriage, Jeff and Melissa both felt they needed a change. "We had two young children to raise," Melissa recalls. "The more we tried to do it in our own strength, the harder it seemed to be. I thought there must be an easier way to raise a family and have a successful marriage."

"My life was filled with all the 'stuff' of this world," Jeff admits. "My priorities were the same as the priorities of this world." The struggles of life had begun to affect their marriage. "We never had drug or alcohol problems, but we had 'me' problems. We felt like something was missing in our lives and in our marriage."

Melissa didn't know yet that a relationship with God was possible. "I did all that I could to hide and avoid any conversations about God—or so I thought," she says. "You can run, but you can't hide!"

Jeff, on the other hand, was starting to sense what needed to change in his life. "Deep down I knew what we needed," he says. "I was brought up in the church, but when I was 17, I just quit going. I was too busy hanging out with my non-Christian friends. I thought I didn't need church or Jesus."

One evening, Melissa was taking a walk with her sister-in-law, Vanessa. It was a moment Melissa says she will never forget. "She began to talk about God and ask me questions that I didn't have answers for," Melissa says. "I remember getting very upset and telling her that, yes, I was a good person. I believed in God, I prayed to Him, and that was all I needed. Boy, was I wrong!"

> ". . . I accepted Jesus as my Savior, hand and hand with my husband here at Calvary Chapel."

Jeff and Melissa continued to grow more and more dissatisfied with their lives. About this time, they discovered that Jeff's sister, Vanessa, and her husband had started attending Calvary Chapel. "On several occasions they invited our children to come to church with them. It was during this time we were in our deepest struggles," Melissa explains.

In January 2000, Jeff and Melissa decided to attend a service at Calvary Chapel. "The first time we came to Calvary Chapel, the Holy Spirit was tugging at my heart," says Jeff. "But during the altar call I sat still. I was afraid to move and afraid I would scare Melissa." Jeff had never spoken to Melissa about God. "I had never even asked her if she believed there was a God."

By the time Jeff and Melissa got home from church that day, Melissa was ready to begin talking about God. Jeff says, "The Lord had begun to do His work! Melissa asked me a question. She wanted to know what it meant to be 'born again.' I explained what it meant. We both talked about it all week and knew that we would go forward during the altar call that next Sunday."

Jeff and Melissa gave their lives to Jesus Christ together as a couple. "On January 23, 2000, I accepted Jesus as my Savior, hand and hand with my husband, here at Calvary Chapel," Melissa says.

Looking back, Jeff now realizes just how much Jesus has changed their lives. "Now we are a team," he says. "Now our priority is Jesus."

"Our marriage is not perfect now," says Melissa. "We still have disagreements, but our focus is not on ourselves or who can win the argument but rather that we have Jesus in our lives. He filled up what was missing. He is the center of our home and our lives."

Jeff, Melissa, and their two children jumped right into the fellowship at Calvary Chapel. "Right away we felt so welcomed and such a part of the ministry," Melissa says. "It was so easy to get plugged in. Vanessa helped by inviting me to a Bible study on how to love your husband. This helped me become more open in prayer and also learn to spend time in the Word."

Jeff and Melissa soon started serving in the children's ministry. Melissa worked with the infants, while Jeff taught the two-year-olds. Later, they taught the second grade class together. Jeff eventually became a head usher, responsible for the Sunday 9 A.M. service. Melissa now works on the church staff.

Spending time together as a family is very important to Jeff and Melissa. One of the ways they keep this a priority is by continuing to worship and serve together. Melissa expresses their new commitment: "As a family, we have come to rely on His strength and His Word daily."

Jeff and Melissa Niven

Chapter 9

Streams in the Wasteland

LANA FRANKLIN

> Forget the former things; do not dwell on the past. See, I am doing a new thing! Now it springs up; do you not perceive it? I am making a way in the desert and streams in the wasteland.
>
> —Isaiah 43:18–19

I grew up a Navy kid, and we moved to Florida when I was 11 years old. At 13, my foundation was shattered when my parents divorced. They remarried each other when I was 14 and then divorced again when I was 15. Needless to say, our home life was completely unstable. After my parents' second divorce, we began to go to church. I can remember going forward many times to confess my sins, but I didn't understand what salvation really meant.

Later on, I began to go to a small church with my neighbor, and it was there that I met my first boyfriend. He was two years older than I was. He went into the military, and we planned to get married after I finished high school. When he announced that he was going to be stationed in Ft. Walton Beach, everything changed. I could not stand the idea of being apart and wanted to get married immediately. My mother did not want me to marry so young, so I threatened to run away if she did not give me permission. She said the only reason she decided to allow me to get married was that *he* seemed to be a good Christian and very responsible. One month after my sixteenth birthday, I was married and on my way to Ft. Walton Beach to begin a new life in the Florida Panhandle.

Exodus 20:12 says, "Honor your father and your mother, so that you may live long in the land the LORD your God is giving you." I did not honor my mother, and the consequences were severe. Within four months, my husband began drinking. He became verbally abusive and punched holes in our trailer walls. I was scared but too proud to call my mom to let her know what was happening.

My husband and I began meeting other military couples and soon entered the party scene. When we were high we didn't fight, so drinking and getting high became a regular part of our weekends. Within three years, my husband was given an honorable discharge for health reasons, and we decided to move closer to my parents. By this time they had remarried each other for the third time.

I was excited and hoped that a new start in Palm Bay, Florida, would end the cycle of drinking and abuse. Once we settled in, we began going to a small church and rededicated our lives to the Lord. Then I became pregnant, and things began to get bad at home again. Although we were very involved in church, our life at home was extremely dark.

By the time our daughter was two years old, my husband had been unfaithful in our marriage. I was horrified and wanted to leave, but the pastor of our church said that I had to forgive him and give him another chance. I submitted and stayed in the marriage, but as time went by, my husband showed no evidence of repentance. He was not open to counseling for his abusive behavior or for his drinking problem.

In 1982 my parents moved to Tennessee, and that summer we went for a visit. During our visit, Mom took us to a revival service. The meeting was held at a large church with stadium seating, and there were more than 1,000 people in attendance. After a time of praise and worship, the pastor turned and pointed directly at me. I was seated about eight rows back and to the left. He said, "Young lady in the red and white dress, come down to the front. I want to pray for you." When I arrived in front he said, "The Lord sees your pain, and He will bring you through." I fell to my knees and began to cry uncontrollably. I was baptized in the Holy Spirit and began speaking in tongues. I knew the Lord had given me the baptism so that I would have His power to persevere in my situation.

I would soon come to understand these words in Isaiah 43:2–3: "When you pass through the waters, I will be with you; and when you pass through the rivers, they will not sweep over you. When you walk through the fire, you will not be burned; the flames will not set you ablaze. For I am the LORD, your God, the Holy One of Israel, your Savior."

In 1984, my parents divorced again, and Mom came back to live in Palm Bay. Then in 1986, the company I worked for offered me a job transfer to Largo, Florida. Our daughter, Angela, was now six years old. My marriage was still a mess, but I thought that this change was an answer from the Lord—a new path to a fresh beginning and a chance to heal my broken marriage.

The move was exciting, but once we settled in, the old ugly issues were still there with us—and now they seemed even worse. My husband was drinking straight whiskey on a daily basis, and the abuse was escalating. At times I would withdraw into my closet to get away from him. I would sit hidden in the deep corner and cry, "God why?" I didn't know how much more I could take. I begged my husband to get counseling, and reluctantly, he agreed. We went for about four months with no change. He later confessed that he went just for show. He didn't believe that he had any problems.

The physical abuse continued, but now my husband was becoming violent towards our daughter. One day, when he pinned her against the wall with his hands around her throat, I drew the line. The counselor suggested that I leave—and I did. My husband continued to threaten and harass us, so I finally sought a divorce.

After 15 years of abuse and betrayal, I became a single mom with a nine-year-old daughter. I felt scared and confused, but mostly angry. I had been going to church and trying to be the responsible one in our marriage. *But where did that get me?* My rebellion against God had begun. I started going out with friends from work and dating, making up for all those lost years.

During this rebellious time in my life, I still felt the importance of teaching my daughter godly values, so I sent her to Christian schools. I was too blind to realize that she needed to be taught those principles by me. I dated the same man for almost three years, but I was devastated when he would not commit to marriage. Our relationship ended. I began to party even more and joined a dating service. Angela would watch me get all dressed up in my little mini-skirts and high heels to go party. She saw her mom for who she really was. I was a hypocrite and felt like a harlot in my soul.

> I was a hypocrite and felt like a harlot in my soul.

When Angela was 13, she began sneaking out of the house with friends and smoking pot. We were both out of control. One night, when I tried to slap her for cussing at me, she caught hold of my hand, and we began to wrestle. I grabbed her, pushed her to the floor, and pinned her down. Before I knew it, I was screaming, crying, and shaking in disbelief at what was taking place. Then something unusual happened. I heard a voice. I knew it was the Lord. He said, "Lana, the battle you are having with your daughter is a picture of the battle you are having with Me." I was crushed. I rolled onto the floor and began to weep uncontrollably. Then I hugged my daughter and asked her to forgive me. I cried out to the Lord for His forgiveness and help.

After that, I decided to give up dating and go back to church. I tried to focus on Angela and regain some sort of control. Soon I was losing the battle and began to feel depressed. I had a friend at the time who couldn't stand to see me down, so she begged me to go out with her. She was a dance instructor and wanted me to meet some of her male friends. She promised me that these men were gentlemen. I relented and went out with her.

One night she introduced me to a man named Ray, who took my breath away. He truly was a perfect gentleman. Later that night, he called my friend and told her that he was going to marry me. The next time we went out, I told Ray that I had just recommitted my life to the Lord and that I would only date a Christian who was interested in marriage. This statement would have scared most men off. Not Ray. He was eager to go to church and ready for a committed relationship. We began dating on August 25, 1994.

Angela continued her downward spiral. I felt that I had absolutely no control. She had seen her mom live a life of hypocrisy, and she didn't trust me or anyone else. When my father and step-mom came to visit, they asked if they could take Angela to live with them for a few months. They wanted to give me time to get my life together, and Dad thought that taking her away from familiar influences would be good for her. I was willing to try just about anything.

Over the next few months, Ray and I became very serious. On February 14, 1995, he proposed. When Angela returned in April, we all enjoyed going to church together. We experienced a time of peace in our household as Angela and Ray developed a friendship. During this time, Ray and I began premarital classes. We were married on June 23, 1995.

We enrolled Angela in a private Christian school while I focused on advancing my career and climbing the corporate ladder. Ray was working at a Mercedes-Benz dealership and doing very well, though he put in long hours and worked most weekends. I soon began to notice he was drinking every night. When I asked him about it, he reassured me that it was just to relax and that he wasn't addicted. I began to sense a problem in our relationship and a growing lack of intimacy. But when I tried to talk to Ray about it, he made excuses and became very attentive—at least for a while.

Against our better judgment, we let Angela return to public school in her junior year. In just a short time, she began to skip class and hang out with the wrong crowd. Her rebellion became so severe that we had to call the police a few times. It felt like we were living a nightmare. We forced Angela to go to a small private school and get her diploma. We told her that she had to get a job or go to college in order to stay at home. She agreed, but her disrespect and abusive behavior eventually led us to make her move out. She struggled and begged to come home.

She promised to go back to college, so we let her move back home and enrolled her in classes.

We purchased a home in Clearwater and changed churches, hoping to get another fresh start. Angela began attending college and seemed to be doing well, but then the roller-coaster ride started all over again. She dropped out of college, started staying out all night to party, and became verbally abusive and disrespectful toward us.

Despite all the chaos at home, I continued to get promoted at work. I was now in sales, working long hours and traveling often. Things became so bad with Angela that we again had to ask her to leave. She moved in with a friend, and within four months called with the news that every mom dreads: "I'm pregnant."

As I processed these words, I fell to the floor and wept bitterly. The news went from bad to worse. The father of the baby was unemployed and selling cocaine. I told Angela she had to give up the baby. Initially, I let my emotions run wild and said that I would pay for an abortion. I was immediately convicted and cried and asked her to forgive me. However, I did encourage her to place the baby for adoption. I felt that at 19, Angela was too irresponsible to be a parent, and *I* was not going to raise her baby.

I took Angela to a few adoption agencies and also to the local pregnancy center. She was determined to keep the baby and raise it herself. I counseled her that if she wanted to be a responsible parent, she needed to get her life straightened out. She began to take the right steps. She went to live at **Alpha, "A Beginning," Inc.**, also known as Alpha House, a transitional home for pregnant, unwed girls. We picked her up each weekend for church, and she rededicated her life to the Lord. Angela delivered a beautiful baby girl in January of 2000 and then came to stay with us until she found a job and saved enough money to get an apartment. She was struggling as a single mom but working hard and taking steps to be a responsible adult.

Ray was very supportive and patient throughout all of these trials, but we still struggled in our relationship. We were going to church, attending classes, and serving, yet still there was no intimacy between us. Ray continued drinking a lot. I tried to figure out what was wrong.

I wondered if my focus on work, Angela, and the baby had caused me to neglect my husband.

Ray left his job selling cars to begin his own business at home. Because my salary was our primary source of income, the timing seemed perfect. I thought, *Maybe this will help our marriage?* Then on Thanksgiving Day 2000, Ray's father died from a sudden, massive heart attack. Ray was badly shaken. He felt compelled to leave the church we had been attending for more than three years. We both desired to find a fellowship that reached out with more compassion for hurting members of the body. We were also intrigued by the teaching style we had experienced once on our visit to a Calvary Chapel in Melbourne, Florida. We were searching for a church where the pastor would teach through the entire Word of God. Ray visited Calvary Chapel St. Petersburg in December 2000 and immediately sensed that he had found the place for us. When he brought me to Calvary Chapel, I also felt at home. We have been attending ever since.

The struggles in our marriage continued. I was making great money but traveling more than ever. When I wasn't traveling, I worked all hours of the night, and then would be gone for two and three days at a time. I was stressed over my job and discouraged with my marriage. I began to feel a desire to stay at home and be a wife to Ray. I wasn't sure how Ray would feel about my quitting, as I generated our sole source of income at the time. So I prayed and then went to Ray. I asked him if there might be a way for me to quit my job and stay at home. His answer amazed me. He said, "If you think this is what the Lord wants you to do, then we need to have the faith that He will provide for us." Even though Ray wasn't earning anything yet in his new business, he spoke with such faith that I felt sure this was the right decision.

When I told my manager that I was thinking of leaving, he said, "You're not going anywhere, Lana. You make too much money!" My manager knew I was a Christian, and I told him that the money did not mean that much to me. I also explained that my husband and my marriage were my priorities. He told me to hold off, and within just a few weeks, the company began announcing layoffs. I volunteered and was blessed with a wonderful severance package that helped to pay our bills for the next year. God had provided for our needs above and beyond what we could imagine!

Now that I was home, I felt I could be a real wife. Within a month, I joined a ladies' **Salt & Light** group at Calvary Chapel. I began to read the Word like never before. My thirst was unquenchable. The Lord spoke to me through every chapter, and I began memorizing Scripture. It was an exciting time. I shared with Ray what the Lord was teaching me and asked him to help me with my memory verses. I became quite the cook and even began to grind wheat and make homemade bread! I also had time to serve in the **Women of Heart** ministry. I was growing spiritually. I thought by becoming a godly wife my marriage would be changed.

After six months, our relationship had not changed at all. I began to cry out to the Lord and ask Him to remove my physical desire for my husband. Emotionally, I could not cope with the lack of affection. "If this is my lot," I prayed, "then God, please fulfill these needs in me." Although Ray was not changing, I began to focus more and more on my relationship with the Lord. He was becoming my only source, my all in all. The Lord helped me to love Ray with a different attitude. When I ministered to Ray, I did it as unto my Lord. It was not easy, but His grace was sufficient for each day.

About a year later, Ray and I were asked to lead a **Salt & Light** couples group at Calvary Chapel. We accepted. Little did anyone realize—including me—that Ray had not yet truly entered into a personal relationship with Jesus. As Ray began to read the Word and memorize Scripture, something started to happen. Things actually got worse at home. I thought the problem was spiritual and suggested we pray for protection. Well, *it was* spiritual all right, but we didn't need to pray for protection. We needed to pray for deliverance.

I can remember the events clearly. It was Good Friday, and I was vacuuming the house. I was overwhelmed with emotion. I began to weep uncontrollably and then fell to my knees in the living room. I didn't know why I was feeling this way, but I began to pray. The Holy Spirit took control, and I prayed and cried for about 30 minutes. *Lord, what is this all about?*

About a week later, I woke up early one morning and felt compelled to get up and check on Ray. When I opened his office door, I was horrified to find him at the computer viewing pornography. I was devastated. After almost seven years of trying to figure out what was wrong with my marriage, I suddenly felt it was all a lie. I didn't want excuses. I didn't want to talk. I wanted out. I wanted a divorce. I felt justified in desiring this. Ray was a liar, a closet drunk, and a porn addict!

I told Ray to leave and went into my bedroom and cried. Before long, I began to hear Ray breaking before the Lord in prayer. My husband was wailing. He was crying out in despair, and I could sense real godly sorrow in his cries. Yet I could not go to him. I was too angry. I surely didn't want to comfort him. I wanted him to experience some of the pain and feel the consequences of his behavior and his sin against me.

Ray did leave later that night, and in the darkness, I cried out to the Lord. I wasn't sure what I was going to do. The pain was horrific. *How could I have married another man who would betray me? Was this now my punishment for the prior divorce and years of rebellion?* I was thinking all sorts of things. I realized I needed to be in the Word. Scripture was my source of comfort and peace. I couldn't tell anyone, because everyone thought Ray was a Christian, including me! I couldn't tell my mom or dad. They would not understand. I had no one to turn to but the Lord. He was my only refuge.

The next day, Ray called to tell me he was staying in a motel by the church and that he had an appointment with one of the pastors. He called the next day, and the next day after that. He told me he was getting counsel from a pastor and was reading and praying. He said he wanted to see me, so I allowed him to come over to talk. When he arrived, he knelt before me and cried and said how sorry he was for hurting me and for destroying our marriage. He confessed that he was an alcoholic and that he was addicted to pornography. He had kept it hidden for years. Then Ray told me that he had been delivered and wanted to serve the Lord with his whole heart. He also said that he didn't want me to forgive him unless the Holy Spirit revealed to me that he had really changed.

Over the next week, Ray continued to take steps to get help. This showed me that he was genuine in his efforts. By confessing his sin and bringing it out in the open, the bondage that had held him captive was broken. Now the Lord could begin to heal our marriage. I let Ray come home, and the slow process of forgiveness and rebuilding trust began. As time went by, we began to forget the former things. We no longer focused on our past. We could see that God was doing a new thing in our lives. He was making a way in the desert and streams in the wasteland for us.

It has been nearly five years since that day when sin was brought into the light. When I look back now, I can say that it has been a truly awesome experience to see the power of our God at work. The Lord changed my bitter heart into a heart of compassion and love. He transformed my husband and restored our broken marriage.

Eventually, Ray and I began to meet other couples at church who were struggling in their marriages. The Lord opened doors for us to counsel with them, which led to teaching group studies on biblical principles for strengthening marriages. Together, we thank God for all He has done in and through our marriage. Privately, I thank Him for His refreshing streams that have healed my heart. *My life belongs to You, Lord. You are worthy of all my praise!*

Lana Franklin

Chapter 10
No Longer a Slave to Sin

RAY FRANKLIN

You have been set free from sin and have become slaves
to righteousness.
—Romans 6:18

I am writing this testimony as a praise offering to the love of Jesus
Christ for a sinner like me and to give thanks to Jesus for bringing
my beloved Lana into my life. I came to truly understand the extent of
God's love only during the last five years. I have realized that His love
was always with me, even when I didn't know He existed. His Spirit
was guiding and protecting me.

As you read my story, you will understand how fitting it is for me
to begin with these words found in 1 Timothy 1:15–17: "Here is a
trustworthy saying that deserves full acceptance: Christ Jesus came into
the world to save sinners—of whom I am the worst. But for that very
reason I was shown mercy so that in me, the worst of sinners, Christ
Jesus might display his unlimited patience as an example for those who

would believe on him and receive eternal life. Now to the King eternal, immortal, invisible, the only God, be honor and glory for ever and ever. Amen."

As a child, I was raised in a denominational church. Although I was taught about Jesus, I didn't have a personal relationship with Him. Instead, I was taught to obey the Ten Commandments or else I would be eternally condemned. My only escape from damnation was to confess my sins to a priest. I wanted to do the right thing, so I confessed my sins over and over again, but I was never freed from the power of sin. In fact, the power of sin grew stronger in my life. I felt the guilt and condemnation of it growing each day. I felt frustrated and doomed.

Eventually, I fled the pain of the church's condemnation. By my first year in high school, if someone had asked me what I believed, I would have answered that I was an agnostic. I sensed there was a power greater than me, but I didn't believe any church knew who the true God was. I certainly didn't believe the church of my childhood held the answers I was seeking. Similar to the children of Israel, I wandered in the wilderness and was a slave to my sinful nature for 40 years.

I started to experiment with alcohol when I was 13 years old and then with drugs when I was in my mid-teens. This helped fuel my lust for women, and I was introduced to the bondage of pornography at a very early age. I was controlled by the lust of my eyes, the lust of my flesh, and the pride of my life. I realize now that although I was trying to run away from God, He never left my side. As I look back, I can remember many instances when His hand of protection was with me, even though my self-destructive nature was putting my life in jeopardy.

In 1968, when I was 19 years old, I enlisted in the Marine Corps, primarily because my dad was a Marine who had fought in World War II. I wanted to follow in his footsteps. I was sent to Vietnam the following year, along with 270 other Marines. On our arrival, two of us were selected for 30 days of mess duty. I was one of the two lucky ones who did not immediately go into the bush. Most of the others in my battalion were assigned to combat and experienced horrific losses during their tour of duty. Many of those Marines never returned home.

At the mess hall, I had the good fortune to have lunch with a Marine MP (Military Police) who mentioned that his unit was looking for recruits with civilian police experience. Although I didn't have police experience, my dad was a New York City police detective, and I felt I had a good story to tell. So the next day, I visited MP Company and told the officer on duty that my dad and my uncle were both policemen and that when I left the Marines I wanted to become a policeman. The officer was so impressed with my story that my orders were changed within a few days. I spent the remainder of my tour in Vietnam as a Division MP, which was a relatively safe place to be.

I don't believe it was just luck that kept me from going into the bush with the other 268 Marines. I believe the Lord protected me on that first day and continued to protect me throughout all of my reckless behavior. While in Vietnam, I did everything within my power to sabotage God's efforts. I smoked pot nearly every day, and when harder drugs were available, I used them as well. I had been introduced to marijuana prior to going to Vietnam, but it became a stronghold in my life while I was there. It remained one long after I returned to civilian life.

I dedicated myself to the pursuit of worldly pleasures, but God did not turn His back on me. He had every right to do so, but He was patient with me. He did not want me to perish without knowing Him. He wanted me to repent and receive Jesus as my Savior. God's mercy continued to protect me many times after I returned from Vietnam. I remember two instances in particular.

The first instance happened while I was at graduate school. I was rock climbing in a gorge with two friends near Ithaca, New York. I had been partying that day, so I was intoxicated, and my climbing experience was very limited. My two buddies, on the other hand, were experienced climbers who wanted to challenge their skills. They quickly left me behind. I was irritated to find myself lagging, so I picked up the pace, only to lose my footing on loose shale.

The next thing I knew, I was sliding on my back down a very steep slope. I rolled over onto my stomach in hopes of slowing my decent, but to no avail. Then out of the corner of my eye, I caught a glimpse of a root just within my reach. I latched onto it with my fingertips. I remember lying there for a minute, trying to catch my breath. Then I turned over and discovered that I had stopped just two feet from a 60-foot drop to the floor of the gorge. Catching that root was my last hope of stopping the fall. I know now I was saved only by the grace of God. Unfortunately, at that time I attributed all of this to my good luck.

The second instance of God's divine protection happened just a few years later. I was driving a Datsun B210 hatchback, one of those very small Japanese cars popular with students. On that day, something extraordinary happened. I was traveling on a one-way road when I noticed a truck on the street ahead barreling toward the intersection at a very high rate of speed. I realized it was not going to stop and that it would T-bone my puny little compact. In the natural realm, my instinct should have caused me to slam on the brakes, but instead I found myself pressing down harder on the accelerator. Seconds seemed to move in slow motion. I remember bracing for the inevitable impact, but to my amazement, the truck passed just behind me.

My first reaction was pure joy because of my good luck. But this time, after reflecting on the impossibility of what had taken place, I realized something greater than luck had occurred. Another force must have caused me to press on that accelerator. I remember wondering if maybe there had been an angel with me that day. In any case, I believe the Lord protected me. God was being patient with me. He did not want me to perish but to repent and receive Jesus. I wish I could say I saw the light and received Jesus on that day, but I did not. I put the episode behind me and continued living in bondage to my sinful nature.

Several years passed. At 33 years of age, I married a woman whose worldly appetites were even greater than my own. My non-Christian friends thought I had it all—a carnal wife, money, and many earthly possessions. But I was dying inside, and I knew it. By God's grace, He intervened seven years later. He helped me begin to seek Him by taking away everything I owned. In the course of four months, the seeds were planted for me to lose the home I was living in, the house I was renting, the sports car I was driving, all the money I had in the bank, and my wife due to her infidelity.

Strangely symbolic of what was happening in my life, the foundation of my house started to erode. A change in the water table caused it to begin to sink into the ground. It was not considered a sinkhole, however, so it was not covered by insurance. The estimates for repairs were approximately $60,000. In my desire to raise this cash, I took the advice of my closest friend regarding a possible takeover of the Home Shopping Network (HSN). My friend was a vendor for HSN and said that his information came from a reliable source within the company.

Although I knew insider trading was illegal, I rationalized that I wasn't really hurting anyone. Besides, I needed the money! So I took all of the cash we had in the bank (around $35,000) and used it to buy HSN stock options. The stock options would expire in three months, but my friend assured me the takeover would happen within that time frame. After two months the takeover still had not taken place, and the options had lost most of their value, but my friend assured me the takeover was just days away. I sold my 300ZX to buy even more stock options.

As you have probably guessed already, no takeover took place, and my worthless stock options expired. I found myself without any liquid assets. As if that were not bad enough, some tenants I had in a house I was renting out vandalized the property prior to leaving. It would require a substantial investment before the house could be rented again, and I

> Although some people believed I was a man of God, I was living a lie.

didn't have it. But my affliction was not yet complete. I learned of my wife's adultery when she called to inform me that she was leaving me. "Oh, by the way," she added, "you need to take the antibiotics I left for you on the kitchen counter."

I lost everything I had depended on for security. Through the loss, God opened a pathway to Him. It didn't happen overnight, but as I lost everything, I slowly began to realize that there must be something more important in life. I began to seek God for the first time since leaving the church of my childhood. I began reading books on spirituality. In my search, I began to see that I needed to have a relationship with God. I remember memorizing Psalm 23 and feeling its power minister to me. I began to pray for the first time in my life. I vividly remember asking the Lord to bring a godly woman into my life, one that would help me know Him better. My prayer was not answered immediately, but three years later, I met Lana. We were married within a year.

I wish I could say that I was transformed immediately, but for the next seven years my sinful nature continued to control me. Although some people believed I was a man of God, I was living a lie. I was more discriminating now, no longer smoking pot, but still drinking several martinis each day. Although Lana sensed my drinking was a problem, she didn't realize the extent of my bondage. She knew nothing of my hidden addiction to pornography.

During this time, the Lord began to witness to me through Lana as she became involved with a ministry called **Salt & Light** at Calvary Chapel. I began to thirst for the changes I saw in Lana as she read the Word and memorized Scripture. Lana shared with me some of what the Lord was saying to her and how He would speak to her and others in the group.

Then, by God's design, Debbie Friley, the founder of the **Salt & Light** ministry at Calvary Chapel, asked Lana and me to lead a group for couples. I agreed to do so, though I knew I was a fraud. However, by agreeing to lead the group, something miraculous happened. I had already read through the Bible several times, but this time I began not only to read the Word but also to ask the Lord to lead me to the scriptures He wanted me to learn. He took me to verses He knew would prepare my heart to receive Him.

Revelation 3:20 was one of the verses that got my attention: "Here I am! I stand at the door and knock. If anyone hears my voice and opens the door, I will come in and eat with him, and he with me." Another was 1 Peter 2:24: "He himself bore our sins in his body on the tree, so that we might die to sins and live for righteousness; by his wounds you have been healed."

When the Lord, in His perfect timing, knew I was ready, He allowed my hidden sin to be revealed. Early one morning, I was in my office in front of the computer looking at pornography. Lana walked in, and at that moment I thought that my life as I knew it was over. In a very real sense it was, but not in the way I imagined. I thought I had lost Lana. She wanted no part of me and the lies I had been living. She wanted to end our marriage. I understood how she felt. I could not imagine how she would ever be able to love me or want to be married to a sinner like me. My heart was filled with regret for the loss of the most important person in my life.

But that day, the Lord revealed something of eternal importance to me. In the midst of my greatest worldly regret, He spoke to my heart and said, "At this moment you feel the pain of separation from the most important person in your life. I want you to imagine the pain and regret you will feel for all eternity if you choose to separate yourself from Me." At that moment, my heart was filled with remorse not only for the sin He revealed to me that morning but also for all of my past sins. In anguish I cried out to the Lord, and He replied with these familiar words: "Here I am! I stand at the door and knock. If you hear my voice and open the door, I will come in and eat with you and you with me."

I fell on my face and yielded my life to God. I have not been the same man since. My journey with Christ began that day. I went to speak with a pastor from Calvary Chapel to confess my sins, and I received godly counsel from Pastor Tim Wolter. He listened as I poured out my heart and encouraged me to get plugged in with other brothers at the church. Soon I became involved with the **Men's Accountability Groups** and also began regularly attending the weekly Men's Breakfast. Over the ensuing months, I developed relationships with other men from the church, and as a result, my relationship with the Lord grew. I also began to spend quiet time with the Lord and read His Word on a daily basis.

Eventually, Tim Hewitt, who was leading the Men's Breakfast at the time, left Calvary Chapel to pioneer a new church. By the grace of God, he asked me to take over facilitating the breakfast, and I have had the privilege of doing this for the last four years. God not only gave me the gift of a wonderful relationship with Him but also restored the relationship with my precious Lana. Together, we are now ministering to other couples through our **Life Group** and through marriage studies that we've been blessed to offer to those who are struggling. I thank God for His grace and mercy in my life and feel privileged to serve the Lord.

It's truly amazing to consider that God would choose to use a sinner like me for His purpose in the lives of others. Yet 2 Corinthians 5:17 explains that we become new creations in Christ. I am living proof of this! Through God's forgiveness in Christ, I am no longer a slave to sin. Second Corinthians 5:19–21 goes on to tell us that we receive the ministry of reconciliation: "And he has committed to us the message of reconciliation. We are therefore Christ's ambassadors, as though God were making his appeal through us. We implore you on Christ's behalf: Be reconciled to God. God made him who had no sin to be sin for us, so that in him we might become the righteousness of God."

My prayer is that this story may be a testimony of God's power to transform a life. If anyone is a slave to sin, he or she need not remain one. I am devoted now to this ministry of reconciliation. My earnest hope is that these words will give others the strength to walk away from sin and discover freedom in Christ.

It is therefore fitting that I end with these words from Psalm 32:1–5: "Blessed is he whose transgressions are forgiven, whose sins are covered. Blessed is the man whose sin the LORD does not count against him and in whose spirit is no deceit. When I kept silent, my bones wasted away through my groaning all day long. For day and night your hand was heavy upon me; my strength was sapped as in the heat of summer. Then I acknowledged my sin to you and did not cover up my iniquity. I said, 'I will confess my transgressions to the LORD'—and you forgave the guilt of my sin."

Ray Franklin

Chapter 11

A Letter From Prison

CHARLES W. LEE

Therefore encourage one another and build each other
up, just as in fact you are doing.
— 1 Thessalonians 5:11

My name is Charles Lee. I've been incarcerated in a Florida
prison for 27 years. My wife, Kathy, and I are servants of our
Lord and Savior, Christ Jesus. We both are members of Calvary Chapel
St. Petersburg.

How we became members of Calvary Chapel is somewhat of a love
story. It's a love story in two ways. First, Kathy and I both love the
Lord and have a passion to do God's work and be involved in ministry.
Second, it is based on the love and support we have received from
many members of Calvary Chapel—people who have shown the love
of Jesus and have opened up their hearts to us.

I'll start by sharing a little of Kathy's story.

When I met my wife almost 20 years ago, she was not involved in a church she could call home. She was doing a lot of church hopping and wasn't comfortable with her spiritual condition. She has always had a strong desire to serve the Lord and be involved in a church where she could use her God-given gifts. At times, Kathy was very discouraged with not having a church family and wondered why she didn't fit in. Nevertheless, I kept encouraging her to seek the Lord and told her He would lead her in the right direction. She didn't know that God was already working things out for her good. He is always working!

In time, Kathy got involved with a local para-church ministry called Single Purpose and started a prison ministry. The group came several times to the prison where I resided. Some of the people were members of Calvary Chapel, a church that Kathy had attended when it first started. Eventually, Kathy found her way back to Calvary Chapel, and it's been her home church ever since.

From what Kathy shared with me, Calvary Chapel sounded like the church in the book of Acts. Worship, praise, and the Word! Right up my alley. Kathy told me about some missionaries to Chad, Africa, named Larry and Janet Gray. Larry had recently come on staff as the missions pastor. I thought to myself that I would love to meet him someday. Well, the Lord does work in mysterious ways. When Pastor Larry heard my story, he was also interested in meeting me. That's where my story begins.

When Kathy became involved in prison ministry at Calvary Chapel, it was arranged for Pastor Larry, as well as the worship group "Barnabas," to hold a service at the prison. After talking with Larry and hearing Barnabas, I was blessed and impressed. It was the first service I had been to in a long time where I really felt like I worshiped the Lord. Inmates talked about that service for weeks!

There aren't words to describe Barnabas. The members of the group are fun loving and a little on the crazy side. But I can also say that they love the Lord, are real, have a passion for ministering to people, and are serious about the Word of God. Kathy and I are proud to call them friends. All of the prisons they have visited really love them, and Barnabas has made a lasting impact on the lives of many inmates and chaplains.

Little did I know that after this encounter I would begin to learn more of what spiritual warfare and faith were all about. I began to struggle spiritually, and my faith in God weakened quickly. The Lord had an inner work to do, and He wanted to use His people from Calvary Chapel to show me His great love, compassion, and faithfulness.

It began when I learned that my mother was dying. Two of my brothers had already gone to be with the Lord, and now this! How could a God who says He loves me allow this to happen? During my years of incarceration, I had prayed that God would keep my mother safe until I came home. Yes, that was my plan, but God had another plan for my life, as well as my mother's. Remember, He is always working.

I was transferred to another institution, and shortly thereafter I received the news that my mother had gone to be with the Lord. At this same time, the Lord sent a man of God back from Africa to proclaim His truth to my wounded soul. Larry Gray was approved for pastoral visits, and he started visiting me monthly. He was there for me during one of the most difficult times of my life and became a trusted friend and mentor. Barnabas came to minister at the prison as well. The group both blessed my soul and gave me reason to sing, "I love the Lord."

> With God working through His people and bringing a man all the way back from Chad to strengthen me, I have faith again.

Since that time, Pastor Danny has welcomed me into the fold. Barnabas is . . . well, let's just say that Barnabas is still Barnabas . . . and Larry and Janet Gray have become dear friends of Kathy and myself. Calvary Chapel has become my family, giving me many brothers and sisters who have supported and believed in me, even without ever meeting me face to face. The church has reached out to me and shown me *agape* love.

With God working through His people and bringing a man all the way back from Chad to strengthen me, I have faith again. Although I may still tremble at times, the Rock of Christ on which I stand will never be moved. My faith in God is more precious than gold and silver or any earthly thing. Now I understand the chief objective for man: "To glorify God and to enjoy Him forever."

I understand Paul's words in Romans 8:38–39 when he said, "For I am convinced that [nothing] will be able to separate us from the love of God that is in Christ Jesus our Lord." If I had to sum up and describe in a word my experience thus far with the people of Calvary Chapel, it would be "Christlike." All praise to the Lord! God is always at work. We must see where He's working and join Him there. Even in prison!

Editor's Note: Charles has been incarcerated since he was 17 years old. He and Kathy were married on September 6, 1993. In November 2006, Charles was transferred to Everglades Correctional Institution, where he is participating in a transitional program. The goal of this program is to prepare Charles for his eventual release back into society. After long years of waiting, this has given Charles and Kathy a renewed hope for their future together. They know their prayers are being answered through the outpouring of support from the members of Calvary Chapel.

Charles and Kathy Lee

Chapter 12 •

Bearing Fruit ~ Bringing Hope

CHRIS AND HEATHER MOELLER
By Mary Fairchild

He will be like a tree planted by the water that sends out its roots by the stream. It does not fear when heat comes; its leaves are always green. It has no worries in a year of drought and never fails to bear fruit.

—Jeremiah 17:8

I met Heather Moeller in the fall of 1999, when she came to Calvary Chapel's church office seeking counsel. We went to my office to talk for just a few moments, and before either one of us had realized, more than half an hour had passed. There was something very genuine about Heather's spirit that caught my attention. It must have been the earnestness of her first love for Jesus shining through. She was a new Christian, just a few months old in the Lord, and she was obviously hungering and thirsting after God. This was something beautiful to observe. And though Heather had come to me for help, I was the one who felt encouraged and refreshed by our time together.

We prayed that day, asking God to save and deliver her husband, Chris. Just a few weeks later, on a Wednesday night, I felt even greater joy as I watched Chris walk into the auditorium from the church lobby, where he had been listening to Pastor Danny on the TV monitor. He went straight to the altar and gave his heart to Jesus. Another new life in Christ was conceived that night. And like two new trees, Chris and Heather began to be planted by the living water, feasting on God's Word, drinking of His Spirit. These two lives would soon begin to bear fruit of their own, just as Scripture promises. I'd like to tell you their story.

Chris and Heather were both raised in broken, abusive homes. "I grew up with very little supervision," says Heather. "I had been abused several times due to neglect. I had tried smoking pot, cigarettes, drinking, and sex by the age of 10. By high school, I was regularly smoking pot, drinking, and doing LSD and [hallucinogenic] mushrooms."

Most of Heather's childhood memories are bleak, but there was one bright spot that stands out in her mind. "There was a lady named Cora who lived across the street when I was about eight years old," she explains. "She told me about the Lord and gave me a Bible. She taught me John 3:16. I think that I probably asked the Lord into my heart back then. As I grew up, I really had strong values about family and about the man being the head of the home. I knew that I only wanted to be married one time."

Chris, on the other hand, remembers few Christian influences during his childhood. "My parents divorced when I was six years old, and soon after, my brother and I moved in with my new step-dad and his five kids," he explains. "In that household, I was introduced to alcohol and drugs of many kinds. Being the youngest of the seven kids, I also learned that fighting was essential to survival, and I did so often. I started smoking pot and drinking when I was 12 years old and was thrown out of middle school for fighting. By tenth grade, I had experimented with most recreational drugs. Violence and drugs had become my identity. In the eleventh grade, I was expelled and was fortunate enough to go to a dropout prevention program and graduate.

"Like most young people who know everything, I couldn't move out of the house quick enough. I got a job fixing air conditioners and moved into an apartment with my two best friends. After a while, I was fired from my job due to a drug test, and I decided it was time to go into full-time drug dealing. Just call me "Einstein!" As you could imagine, I lived the fast life: money, parties, and total craziness—never even considering God's existence at the time, or the fact that He was protecting me."

When Chris and Heather met, she was working in a bar and had begun using cocaine and drinking heavily. "I look back on God's grace that I am alive today, because almost every night I drove home under the influence and very intoxicated." As Chris and Heather's dating relationship progressed, so did their drug habits. "It soon wasn't fun anymore," Heather says. "Our habit spiraled out of our control. Our supplier would no longer deal to us; he said we were out of control. It seemed like problems were everywhere. Finally, we went up to North Carolina to try to get away from it all. When we came back home, we decided that we were going to try to start over. I had begun working for a physical therapy office, and Chris had gone back to repairing air conditioners. We were still going out and partying all the time, going to the bars every night, but we had stopped doing cocaine."

On Christmas Day 1996, Chris and Heather were engaged. Then about one week later, Heather discovered she was pregnant. "When I found out I was pregnant, my life changed," she says. "I stopped smoking and drinking. It was now time to really grow up." Chris and Heather married when she was nine months pregnant, 28 days before their daughter, Emily, was born. As new parents, they struggled. "Chris was introduced to painkillers when Emily was about one year old," says Heather. These prescription drugs would later prove to be the most stubborn of Chris's addictions. As a new couple, they also struggled in their marriage. "I wanted him to grow up and be responsible," says Heather. "We had been to three different marriage counselors, but no one helped. We were barely hanging on."

When Emily was a baby, Chris's cousin invited the Moellers to Calvary Chapel. Each later admitted that they were probably looking for an excuse to leave that first time, and they ended up walking out of the service. However, about a year later, the seed that had been planted in childhood began to stir in Heather's heart. The couple decided to accept another invitation to Calvary Chapel. "It was in June of 1999 when we finally came. I knew right away that this was where I needed to be, but I didn't really start getting serious with the Lord until July," explains Heather. "I remember I told Chris, 'This is it. This is how I want to live my life.'"

Looking back, Heather says, "I'd been so many places, and I'd tried many different roads. I had been promiscuous and tried lots of drugs. When I was in high school I tried to fit in with every group, but I just knew when I came into this church that these people had something that I wanted. I realized it was Jesus . . . I gave my life to the Lord on July 4, 1999. I finally found my purpose in life. I knew God would heal the pain of my past. I felt like a weight had been lifted."

> ". . . I just knew when I came into this church that these people had something that I wanted. I realized it was Jesus . . . "

Chris was not so eager. "I remember the first time we came to church . . . I fought it with all I had. I think my fingernail marks are still outside the doors," he says. However, as they continued to attend regularly, Chris began to notice a difference in Heather. "She just took off with the Lord, whereas I was still having problems with drugs," he says.

Chris's addiction was so severe that Heather was contemplating giving up on the marriage. "I was at the point where I really didn't care whether I had my husband or not. We were both ready to call it quits." But Heather didn't give up. She began to pray and read God's Word. One day, she simply refused to think about divorce as an option. "Chris didn't like it at first," she says. "He would yell at me, and I just stopped arguing with him. I kept reading that verse in 1 Peter 3 about wives being submissive, and you'll win your husbands over with your gentle spirit. The Lord knew exactly when I was ready to give up, and so He just kept showing me His Word and helping me to stay married to this person that I sometimes hated."

Heather began to go to a Bible study and meet friends who would encourage her. "All of the women were very friendly and not judgmental about my situation—so different from the world," she says.

"They encouraged me to seek God and not to just leave my husband. I was always very independent. Yet I wanted a husband who would take on the role of the man. I was just afraid I wouldn't be taken care of." Heather began to trust God to take care of her needs. "I read the Word every single day," she says. "For the longest time, I spent every moment that I could reading the Word. I prayed and asked the Lord to give me a teachable heart and give me a desire for the Lord. And even when I didn't have a desire, He gave me that desire for Him."

One day in November 1999, Heather felt the Lord leading her to fast for Chris's salvation. "That was such a special day with the Lord. I was just floating," she says. Little did she know that on that very night while she was in church, Chris had arrived late and was sitting in the lobby.

"I had gotten there late and was watching the service from the lobby," Chris recalls. "That day was just a normal day, but the message hit me like a rock. So many times before I had wanted to get up and go up and confess, but I just didn't. That night I was in awe thinking, *I do not want to go to hell and spend eternity there.* I had always believed in God, but I never thought of Him as a personal God. I never thought that God loved me, since He had much more important people than me to deal with. I never considered the power of God; I just didn't think about it." Suddenly, it hit him that night that he could die tomorrow and go straight to hell.

Even after his salvation, Chris still battled with his addiction, though he desperately wanted to be free. "One night, after a Wednesday night service, I just sat up at the altar and cried because I couldn't stop doing drugs," he says. "I thought everything in my life would get better, but it didn't. Pastor Frank Dehn came and talked to me because I was crying. We prayed together that the Lord would change my heart and put me in the right direction."

A short time later, the Lord brought Chris to a point of crisis. "The next month, while doing drugs, I wrecked my company truck, and everything exploded in my life," he says. Chris experienced the love and support of his brothers and sisters during this time when he needed it the most. "A key person God has used in my life since coming to the Lord has been Pastor Frank Dehn," Chris says. "Through all my troubles, I was supported and firmly encouraged by Pastor Frank and his trusty sidekick, Tom Teel. Now, anyone who knows these guys knows you ain't gettin' away! Even knowing that I was struggling with a drug addiction, they continued to love me in that Frank and Tom sort of way."

Others upheld Chris in prayer as well. "Glenn Temme prayed with me every day, and Pastor Vivian [Laird], he prayed with me too," says Chris. "I mean, everyone here at Calvary Chapel, whether they know it or not, has said something to me that has really stuck with me. Cindy Neidert told me one day how much it encouraged her to see me growing. I just said, 'Wow!' You don't think people notice, but they do."

Chris and Heather faced enormous challenges during their first few years as believers. "After the Lord delivered me from that nasty cocaine habit, my dependence on prescription pain killers grew out of control," Chris says. "There were periods of time that I was clean here and there, but there was no heart change. I had to be broken."

> "There were periods of time that I was clean here and there, but there was no heart change. I had to be broken."

Shortly after Chris was saved, God gave Heather a vision to prepare her for the tough road ahead. "Chris was sitting on the couch, and I was kneeling in front of him, looking up at him reverently," she recalls. "And the Lord said, 'You will minister as you have been ministered to.' Second Corinthians 1:3–5 says, 'Praise be to the God and Father of our Lord Jesus Christ, the Father of compassion and the God of all comfort, who comforts us in all our troubles, so that we can comfort those in any trouble with the comfort we ourselves have received from God. For just as the sufferings of Christ flow over into our lives, so also through Christ our comfort overflows.' I understand this better now. At the time, I didn't really know what that meant. Over the next four years, I would learn what it meant to be comforted by God.

"For the next year, Chris seemed to do pretty good," says Heather. "He went on a mission trip, was involved in **Men's Accountability Groups**, and we even started going to a **Life Group**. But after a while,

I noticed him withdrawing from church and fellowship. I found out he was using again, and before long it was worse than before." Heather took refuge in God's Word. She meditated on God's promise in Philippians 1:6 that He would complete the work He had begun in Chris's life. Heather says, "I think for a long time I wanted Chris to be clean so we could be that 'smiley church-going couple.' But God wanted us both to be in love with Him. God was looking for devotion at all cost."

By the summer of 2002, Chris and Heather had two more children. "I really wanted a godly husband," Heather says. "But God wanted Chris's heart. Things were spiraling down fast. I never knew when I would have money for groceries or to pay the bills. I was bouncing checks, and the bank closed our account. We had at least one utility shut off every month for over a year. I stopped asking for my will to be done and asked God to save Chris from himself. I loved Chris so much that I gave him to the Lord. I stopped fighting the battle in my flesh."

Chris described his last year as an addict. "I had built up a huge tolerance to the pills, so I had to take about 40 a day—whether it be Vicoden, Percocet, Oxycontin, it didn't matter. And if I couldn't get the pills, methadone and heroin were not out of the question. All of our money was going to feed this horrible addiction. I spent little time with my family, because I was constantly searching for drugs. It had consumed me. I was tired. I was unhealthy. I was ashamed of who I was. I missed my family.

"It was through my wife that the Lord really blew me away. Through all the hell I put her through, she held on to the Lord with a gentle, quiet, submissive spirit. She prayed for me, she supported me, she encouraged me. She loved me no matter what. I knew something had to be done.

"I cried out to God. I wanted out, but I could not do it on my own. I knew the opiate withdrawals would be too much. So I asked God to show me a way out. He did just that. I was soon confronted by a brother at church about my drug addiction. I tried to lie to him and tell him everything was fine, but the Lord touched my heart that night. Within 20 minutes of his leaving my house, I had to call him and confess. This was a major turning point in my life."

After prayer and careful consideration, the Lord provided a way in August 2003 for Chris to go to a place called **Calvary House**, a ministry of Calvary Chapel Fort Lauderdale. The **Calvary House** program is an intense discipleship ministry for men with addictions that requires a 10 to 12 month commitment from participants.

Chris had to complete a detoxification program before he could enter **Calvary House**, but he didn't want to undergo the usual methadone detoxification method. At the time, Operation PAR (Parental Awareness Responsibility) just happened to be starting a new detox drug trial that typically took three to four weeks to complete and had minimal side effects. After just one week in the program, Chris had weaned himself off the trial drug and was ready to join **Calvary House**. Once there, he would begin the fiercest battle of his life.

In the meantime, the Lord provided support for Heather and their children. "The same brother who confronted me with my sin offered his home," says Chris. "My wife and three children moved in with his wife and four children. I will never forget the day I walked out the door and looked back into my wife's bedroom, and she held the children, crying. It was so painful, but now I realize it was perfect. I was a broken man."

Although Chris entered the **Calvary House** program a broken man, he would come out a new man. "It was at **Calvary House** where the Lord changed my life," he says. "During my time there, the Lord delivered me from drugs. He showed me that He is real and alive and that He has a plan for my life. I knew there was no turning back. I would now live my life for the Lord, Jesus Christ. It was also there at **Calvary House** that the Lord gave me a new love for my beautiful wife and children. I had a new desire to be a godly husband and father."

Heather soon began to see a new Chris—the man she'd always wanted. "It was amazing for me to see God transforming my husband into this godly man," she says. "He was so humble and kind to me." Yet deep in her heart where the trust had been destroyed, she needed time and God's grace to repair the damage. "After Chris came home from **Calvary House**, I struggled the first year with trust. In my mind I knew God had delivered Chris, but my heart was still hurting from the lies and deception of the past. Chris was very patient with me, always reassuring me that he had been delivered and that he was walking with God."

Chris and Heather have experienced God's healing power of reconciliation as He has transformed their lives. Chris says, "After returning home, I had a job waiting for me, and Heather and I found a house within two weeks. The Lord truly blessed our lives. Since then our marriage, our children, and our lives have been an amazing joy."

"God gave me back love for my husband," says Heather. "The Lord is just amazing—the grace that He has given me to really trust Chris."

After Chris came home from **Calvary House**, he and Heather began hosting a **Life Group** in their home and serving in several ministries. Two of these ministries are very near to their hearts. Chris feels honored to minister every Tuesday night to the men at **Calvary House** in St. Petersburg, a discipleship program for men with addictions that is similar to the one he attended in Fort Lauderdale.

God brought to fruition the vision He had given to Heather years earlier. "Chris and I co-lead the Friends and Family support group of the **Most Excellent Way**," says Heather. The **Most Excellent Way** is a ministry of Calvary Chapel that helps people become free from addictive, compulsive, and life-controlling behaviors. The Friends and Family group offers support to those who suffer alongside the addict. "We are ministering to others as we have been ministered to," says Heather. "I am able to share what I have learned about God's character and how He brought me through tough times. It's about focusing your eyes on Christ, not on the addict." Chris is able to minister to people from the addict's perspective. He says, "I can talk about how self-absorbed addicts become, how oblivious they are to their loved ones, and how unaware they are of the addiction's effect on their family and friends."

Today, Chris and Heather have been married for nine years. Chris has been drug-free since August 2003, and together they have established a hope-filled home of five happy children. Their lives testify of miracles. Fruit has borne fruit. God's power has demonstrated hope giving birth to hope, and they are comforting others with the same comfort they have received from the Lord.

Chris and Heather Moeller

The Moeller Family

Chapter 13

A New Song to Sing

DAN CLARK

> I waited patiently for the LORD; he turned to me and heard my cry. He lifted me out of the slimy pit, out of the mud and mire; he set my feet on a rock and gave me a firm place to stand. He put a new song in my mouth, a hymn of praise to our God. Many will see and fear and put their trust in the LORD.
>
> —Psalm 40:1–3

A long time ago, when I was still living with my parents, I thought I gave my life to Christ. I went to church with my family almost every Sunday and carried a Bible with me, but I only opened it when the pastor told us to look up a verse for that day's sermon. After I graduated from high school and entered college, I began pulling away from God. In fact, I turned my back on Him completely, even to the point of claiming to be an agnostic.

I was married after college, but that marriage ended in failure. I next lived alone in an apartment and did the bar scene. I was looking in all the wrong places for the woman of my dreams. Finally I got tired of it. I basically gave up and decided I was not going to look for anyone.

One day—it happened to be a Sunday—I was walking back to my apartment from the 7-Eleven and happened to walk near the apartment pool. Previously, I had decided that I was not interested in the pool, so I had stopped going there. But this day was different. This day as I walked past, I heard the voice of the Lord speaking to me. He was speaking in the only language I understood to be His—King James. I believe strongly that God talks to us in ways that get our personal attention—ways that let us know it is Him because of how He says it or what He says. I distinctly heard Him say, "Get thee to the pool!"

> I believe strongly that God talks to us in ways that get our personal attention—ways that let us know it is Him because of how He says it or what He says.

That made sense to me at the time. My knowledge of God was limited to the very little I had read in a King James Bible so many years ago, and then, only occasionally on Sundays.

Of course I said, "No, I'm not going to the pool!" I proceeded to walk to my apartment. Well, God wouldn't let it go. He kept saying the same thing over and over: "Get thee to the pool!" And I kept saying, "No." Well, I finally relented, changed into my bathing suit and headed over to the pool.

When I got there, the pool was very crowded. There were only two chairs available. One of them had a towel on it, but the other did not. So I went over and put my towel on the empty chair and lay down. I wasn't planning to talk to anyone but just take a nap. A few minutes later, a lady I did not know came up and sat on the chair next to me, the one with the towel. Out of courtesy, I leaned over and asked her if the chair I was in had been in use by her or a friend. "No," she said. So I lay back and closed my eyes, intent on being alone.

A couple of minutes later, the lady started talking to me. I said to myself, *Well, there goes my nap* and began talking with her. She said that she was only going to be there for a few minutes, as she had to go to work in a little while. I asked her where she worked that she would be going in on a Sunday afternoon. When she said, "Shoney's," I laughed. At first she was offended at my response, but I quickly explained that I had been a manager for Shoney's restaurant. So we had something in common.

Well, one thing led to another, and we became friends, and about a year later we were married. I believe that meeting Jo, my wife, that day was purely a God thing! He had given her to me when He told me to go to the pool. He had arranged for that one empty lounge chair to be next to her. If I had not listened to God, I most likely would have never met her.

Over the years I had become devoted to alcohol, drugs, and pornography. Even though I was now married to a woman God had given me, I was still intent on living in sin. I began to think that if I lived alone, I could still sin all the time. Jo tried to put up with me and hung in there for me, but I ignored her and asked for a divorce. At that time, we had been married for 12 years. After several more months, we finally did get a divorce. I moved into my own place and sank deeper and deeper into my pit of sin.

One weekend, about a year later, after a few days of drinking and smoking pot, I hit rock bottom. I wanted to kill myself. If I had not given my shotgun to my brother earlier that year, I probably would have. During those miserable hours, my ex-wife, Jo, showed up at my door and said that the Lord had told her she needed to come to me right away, because I was in trouble. She had been at work when the Lord told her this and had left immediately. I wasn't answering my phone and had not shown up for work that day. Jo convinced me that I needed to go to the hospital. There, I recovered and was out in a few days.

After that experience, Jo said that I should start attending church again. I told her fine, I would go to church with her, but I didn't want to go to a church where we had to "do" anything. So, for a couple of weeks we went to one of those churches where you stand, kneel, say a few words, and then go home. That church seemed dead, even to me. I was getting nothing from going there.

Jo then suggested that I attend Calvary Chapel with her. She had been a regular, more or less, since the early days when the church met in the warehouse. The entire time we had been married and living in St. Petersburg I had never gone to church with her. In my old days, I welcomed the opportunity to be alone so I could get high. I had no friends other than a few acquaintances from work.

So I started coming to Calvary Chapel with my ex-wife. During one of Pastor Danny's sermons, the Lord spoke to me. I came down front at the end of the service, knelt before the Lord, and dedicated my life to Jesus. I asked Jesus to forgive me for my sins and my wasted life. I asked Him to come back into my life and heart. I was born again on that day, October 13, 2002. I remember the sermon as well. It was about how Jesus is the shepherd looking for His lost sheep. He was ready to take me back, despite my sin and all of my imperfections. In that instant, I knew I had received eternal life and was changed forever!

> As I write this, we are going on two and a half years of our second marriage together. God gave my wife to me for a second time!

When I came down front, I was crying. I was broken and needed the Lord. One of the prayer counselors talked to me. I am sorry that I do not remember his name, but he did a wonderful thing for me. He suggested that I get into a small group and perhaps attend a **Men's Accountability Group** meeting. He also told me whom to call about getting involved in the group. Later that week, I called Tim Thompson, the leader of the **Men's Accountability Group**. I started attending regularly and soon became a small group leader.

Two months after I was born again, Jo and I were remarried. As I write this, we are going on two and a half years of our second marriage together. God gave my wife to me for a second time! I thank the Lord for her faithfulness. I thank the Lord for sending her to me that day when I needed her so. And I thank the Lord for causing her to ask me to come back to church. Most of all, I thank the Lord for sending me to the pool that day so many years ago!

In my youth, I played the guitar, but I had not even touched one for more than 23 years. Because I love music, I wanted to learn some of the songs we were singing in church. Then I found out about the third annual Worship Workshop in the Woods that was being held in February 2003. It was a workshop about worship, with an emphasis on guitar playing. At that workshop, I asked God to forgive me for burying my talents and to give me back my musical gift. Guess what? He did! He has guided my path to this day. Now, not only am I singing and playing music, but also God is giving me original songs to share with others! I have also attended every worship workshop since 2003.

In June 2003, a few months after the workshop, Jo was at a Bible study, and I was at home playing my guitar. Suddenly, a couple of chords came to me that sounded pretty good. So I prayed to the Lord right then and there to give me a new song. I had not written any music for over two decades. I told the Lord that if He wanted to give me the words to a song, I would open my Bible to the book of Psalms. Well, when I opened my Bible to a random place in Psalms, the words on the two open pages did not seem to fit the music. So I figured I would turn one page, and when I did, there were the words! They are found in Psalm 40:1–3.

God is so great! He had given me my first new song in more than 23 years, and the words were so appropriate for my life! I am now using the gifts God has given me. I lead praise and worship at the **Men's Accountability Group,** along with another guy who attends Calvary Chapel. I've also become involved in music groups that bring the Word of God in song to nursing homes, several **Life Groups**, St. Vincent de Paul Homeless Shelter, and other places as God leads me.

On April 15, 2005, at age 52, I reached another milestone in my life. I finished reading through the entire Word of God for the first time ever! And, of course, I've already started on the second go round!

Today, I am a totally different person than I used to be. I am happy with life, I have God with me again, and I have my wife back again. Jo and I are happier than we have ever been, because we are truly one together in the Lord as He intended for us to be. We are also blessed to have a small group meeting in our home. I have more friends than

I have ever had in my life, and they are Christian friends! I try to serve the Lord to the best of my ability. But most important of all, I know that if I were to die today, I would have eternal life and go to heaven!

Dan Clark and his wife, Jo

Chapter 14
No Longer a Number

ELIZABETH JACQUIER AND DIANE SOSNOSKI

So in Christ we who are many form one body, and each
member belongs to all the others.
—Romans 12:5

*Editor's Note: The following story is actually two testimonies, submitted
by two different women, Elizabeth Jacquier and Diane Sosnoski. Both
women heard God's voice and eventually obeyed. Their stories weave
together, creating a beautiful picture of the body of Christ and how each
member belongs to the others.*

Elizabeth: I was living in Pennsylvania in 2003, when God called
me. I was alone one afternoon in my house, and I heard a strong
voice. I looked around, but I didn't see anyone. The television in my
living room was on, but I couldn't hear it. When I tried to get up to
fix the TV, I discovered that I couldn't move. I felt numb. The next
moment I heard the strong voice say, "Your mission is to contact the

people and help." I was shocked. I looked around to the right and to the left, but nobody was there. I wanted to get up but couldn't. I felt glued to the couch.

Two hours later, the sound of the television came back, and I found that I could move again. I thought to myself, *O Lord, what does "contact the people and help" mean? And how am I going to do this? I don't know anyone.* At the time, I was living alone. My husband had died. So I said to the Lord, "Okay, I ask You to work in my life. I give myself completely to You."

One year later, I moved to Florida. I didn't know anyone, not even a few people. I was so hungry for God and wanted to go to church, but I didn't know who to ask. Finally, I met some neighbors who took me to their church, but it was a distance away. I had always prayed that the Lord would give me a church near my home, because I don't like to drive. I also wanted to find a church where I felt comfortable, like being in a family.

I visited a few nice churches, but I didn't feel like they were my home. One day, I went with my neighbor to the store. On the way home, we passed Calvary Chapel, and I noticed that the parking lot was packed. I asked my neighbor, "What kind of church is Calvary Chapel?"

"Oh, forget that church," my neighbor replied. "It is charismatic." I thought, *Okay, I think I will visit. It sounds like it could be good for me.*

The next Sunday I went to Calvary Chapel. When I entered, looked around, and saw everyone leaving from the 9 A.M. service, I started to panic. I thought I had missed the service! Then I thought, *No one is going to come to the 11 A.M. service.* But soon, it was packed as well. I listened to the music and began to feel like this could be my home church.

I attended services on Wednesdays and Sundays week after week and month after month, but I still didn't know anyone. I would just watch the people and drink the coffee. I started feeling sad, because I liked the church very much, but I didn't know a soul and didn't have any friends. So in September, I decided that if I didn't meet someone at this last service, I would go to another church.

Diane: I was walking out of the Sunday service into the lobby one Sunday in September when the Holy Spirit told me to go and talk to a woman that I saw sitting in a chair. I wish I could say that I said, "Yes, Lord," and immediately went and talked to her, but I didn't. To be honest, I was not in a good mood that day and didn't want to talk to anybody. I reminded the Lord that I don't always know what to say to people and that I'm not very good at carrying on a conversation.

The Lord and I went back and forth for a while. Finally, I told the Holy Spirit that I was going to the ladies restroom and that if the woman was still sitting there when I came out, I would go up and speak with her.

Elizabeth: When I went to the service that day, it seemed as if Pastor Danny was speaking right to me. He said, "You can't be just a number in this church. You must get involved." I thought to myself, *How does he know this about me?* I realized that I was just a number. I had been simply coming and going, coming and going. I became very sad, because I knew I was alone and still didn't know anyone. So I decided to stay after church and have a cup of coffee. While I sat drinking my coffee, I closed my eyes and prayed, "Lord, You know I am all alone here. Please send someone to me. I don't know what to do."

Diane: All the while I was in the restroom, I was struggling with what to say to the woman I didn't know. When I came out, she was still sitting there. I again reminded the Lord that He would have to give me the words to say, because I didn't want to do it. Then I approached the woman, took a deep breath and said, "Hello. Are you alone?"

Elizabeth: As soon as I finished the prayer, I put my coffee down and looked up. A woman was standing there. She said, "Hello. Are you alone?"

I said, "Yes! I am alone!"

Then she asked, "Can I sit near you and talk with you?" I thought, *Oh my God, I just prayed. I didn't even have the words in my mouth and yet You knew them!* It was just as Psalm 139:4 said: "Before a word is on my tongue you know it completely, O LORD."

Diane: After that, I really didn't have to worry about what to say next. Elizabeth began pouring her heart out and sharing about how she had just prayed for the Lord to send her someone. Wow! Talk about being humbled!

Elizabeth: So, this woman came up to me and we sat together and we talked. I told her that I was just a number. Her name was Diane, and while she was sitting there with me, she saw her friend Brooke Donnelly, who had stopped in front of us to talk with someone. Diane got up and brought Brooke over, and Brooke was very happy to meet me. So I also told her my story of how I felt I was just a number. We all prayed together, and they told me about a **Salt & Light** dinner that was being held the next day. I explained that I didn't think I would be able to find it, so Diane offered to give me a ride.

> I was a number, but I am not a number anymore. I am somebody in Jesus Christ's body!

When I went to the **Salt & Light** dinner the next day at Pattie Cleberg's house, I met 10 people! It was a great time in my life. That day I learned of two **Salt & Light** groups. One was right near my home, while the other one was on Madeira Beach. I attend both of them now on Wednesdays, one at 10 A.M. and the other at 3 P.M. Then I go to the evening service at Calvary Chapel. I have a full day!

I have met so many people. I finally realize what God meant when He said to me, "Contact the people and help." I was a number, but I am not a number anymore. I am somebody in Jesus Christ's body! And I want to glorify God for this.

Diane: It brought tears to my eyes to think how God used me in answering a prayer from this woman's heart. And it made me wonder, *How many times will it take for the Lord to get our attention to be obedient? How many blessings will we miss out on because we don't listen to His voice?*

Diane Sosnoski and Elizabeth Jacquier

Chapter 15
Delivered from Darkness

BROOKE DONNELLY

> But you are a chosen people, a royal priesthood, a holy
> nation, a people belonging to God, that you may de-
> clare the praises of him who called you out of darkness
> into his wonderful light. Once you were not a people,
> but now you are the people of God; once you had not
> received mercy, but now you have received mercy.
> —1 Peter 2:9–10

In May 1996, I was living as a lesbian with my girlfriend in Hollywood, California, when the Lord dramatically took hold of my life. Let me back up just a bit, though, and tell you the story.

I met my girlfriend while living in Detroit, Michigan. She had moved into the apartment next door. She introduced me to the underground punk scene. I discovered this new world was violent and had strong demonic influences that offered me a position of power. This appealed to me, because during my younger years my personal rights had been stripped from me through years of sexual abuse.

In the punk club where we hung out, I felt that no one could hurt me anymore. I was "in" with the group that ran the place. I soon conformed to a life of violence. I became a bouncer in the club and was treated with respect because of it. After my first fight, I was congratulated and treated like a celebrity. I was addicted. I loved the feeling of power.

When my next-door neighbor and I began our lesbian relationship, nothing in the world mattered to me but her. She became my life, and we were inseparable. We were known as a couple, both in the punk clubs and in the gay clubs. We were making a name for ourselves in Detroit, but this was not enough for us. We were both addicted to the attention we received because of our wild looks.

In 1993, we headed for Hollywood to pursue our next venture of becoming rich and famous. A few days after we arrived, my girlfriend decided that it was time to investigate the new scene we were set on conquering. Her plan was to go into West Hollywood and learn who it was we needed to know. So we set out one night, wearing our leather jackets, combat boots, and baseball hats. We could have easily been mistaken for guys, which is exactly what two gang-bangers did. As we passed by the payphone they were using, they hung up and started walking right behind us.

As they continued their pursuit, we both sensed that we were in danger. We walked numbly, in silence. I grasped the chain in my pocket and thought of trying to hit one of them in the face, but I was way too scared. So instead I said a small prayer: "Lord, please help!" God heard me and answered my prayer. I immediately felt a rush of heat come down the back of my legs. The two guys stopped following us and veered off into the parking lot. We continued to walk, and my girlfriend blurted out, "Did you just feel that heat?" I couldn't believe that she had felt it too, so I exclaimed to her that I had just prayed. We walked down the street thanking God. At the time, I remembered a verse that my mom had taught me as a child from Romans 10:13: "Everyone who calls on the name of the Lord will be saved."

Another night, after returning from a club with our roommate, my girlfriend and I were met by a couple that lived in the same building.

The girl had come to our door a few times already, high on crack, and would ask questions about what it was like to be a lesbian. This night, as we waited for the elevator, her boyfriend grabbed our roommate and threw her into the open elevator. He called her a dyke, among other choice words, and repeatedly punched her in the face.

My girlfriend jumped in the elevator to help, while I stood outside watching. Then I decided to jump in and help as well. I got knocked against the wall and my elbow hit the button for the basement. We started to descend. The next thing I knew, I was being hit in the face, something I had never experienced. The elevator door opened, and we piled out into a cement room at the sub-parking level.

The guy who had been hitting us was the last one out of the elevator. He reached into his back pocket, looked each of us in the eyes and said, "I'm going to kill you." I knew that he was serious, so I decided to pray the same prayer that had helped me before: "Lord, please help!" In the next instant, the man reached out his hand to us and said, "I would like you to accept my apology." We all stood staring at his hand, bewildered. My girlfriend refused to shake his hand, and we all piled back into the same elevator. We traveled up to our floor in silence, got off the elevator, and went into our apartment. I then told them that I had just prayed.

In the meantime, my girlfriend and I continued to explore the gay scene of Hollywood and meet many interesting people. Some were actors and producers, and some were even famous. We again began to make a name for ourselves in the clubs and soon were part of an influential group. This group's number one drug of choice was crystal meth (methamphetamine), and soon we were doing it.

One day, my girlfriend and two other friends went with me to visit my younger sister, Rachel, at her school. She was attending Calvary Chapel Bible School in Twin Peaks, California. When I met Rachel that day, she confronted me with Scripture about the way I was living. I became angry and told her that she would have to choose between me and God's Word. She chose God's Word. I told her that from that day on she was on my blacklist. She went back to school crying, but soon got the whole school to start praying for me.

Shortly after, my girlfriend and I went to the store late one night to buy cigarettes. A man who looked homeless sat on the ground outside of the store, crying. We both stopped and asked him what was wrong. He said that someone had given him a card with an angel pinned to it, and it had made him cry. When I looked into his teary eyes, I was overwhelmed with thoughts about Jesus. He was all I could think about. This had never happened to me before. I didn't quite know what to think, except that I suddenly wanted to find Jesus and never leave His side. In my heart I said this prayer to the Lord: "I will follow You wherever You want me to go."

We all sat on the ground around the corner from the store and talked. The man asked us questions, and we responded with truthful answers. Normally we would try to get around the truth, but this man didn't let us. Then he looked at me and said, "You are going to grow your eyebrows back." Shaving my eyebrows was part of my punk look. I adamantly told him I would not, but he insisted. Then he looked at me again and said, "You are going to leave her." This time I didn't say a word. My girlfriend looked at me. She was fuming. I don't know why I didn't respond to him. Before I met him, I had never considered leaving her.

Not long after this, I came to the end of my rope. It was around 11 P.M., the time we usually went to the club, and I was sitting across from my girlfriend at our kitchen table. She had received a flyer inviting us to a new club, but when I saw it, I immediately had the impression that we shouldn't go. My girlfriend, however, insisted that we should go. I kept telling her that I had a bad feeling about it. So she slid the flyer to the middle of the table and said, "Let's just sit on the fence about it." I had never heard her use this phrase before. In fact, the only time I had ever heard it was in church!

All of a sudden, I felt a presence enter the room. It felt like it was coming toward me. I looked around to see what I had felt, but nothing was there. I held out my hand in the direction I felt it coming from and started saying, "In the name of Jesus! In the name of Jesus! In the name of Jesus!" My girlfriend got up and left the apartment. When she left, the presence departed as well.

I stood up from the table and prayed, "Lord, I don't know what You want, but I'm asking You to help me." After I had prayed this prayer, I felt an urgency to leave the apartment. So I left, not knowing where I was going. I ended up at the entrance to the freeway, where I heard the Lord say, "Fear not, for I AM the Lord your God. Though you may walk through the valley of the shadow of death, My rod and My staff will comfort you."

I went down a ravine, out of sight from the traffic above. There, my eyes fixed on a tiny tree, and I heard the words, "Love is the most powerful source in the universe." I made my way toward the tree, and when I was standing under it I heard the same words again. I held one of its leaves and noticed that it was in the shape of a heart. In fact, all of the leaves on the tree were shaped like hearts! I began to cry and said, "Okay, Lord, love is the most powerful source in the universe. But what about my girlfriend?"

> I had to choose who I was going to follow: my girlfriend or Jesus. So I made the decision with my whole heart and chose Jesus.

I clearly heard a loud, "No!" This answer from the Lord allowed me to think clearly for a moment, and when I did, I realized that I had just asked God about my lesbian lover! At that same time, I felt as if someone had walked down into the ravine and was standing behind me. I was so scared and wanted to run away from it all, but I had come to a place of decision. I had to choose who I was going to follow: my girlfriend or Jesus. So I made the decision with my whole heart and chose Jesus. When I did, the presence behind me left!

A few weeks later, I was able to escape from Hollywood. I went home to my parents, who were living in South Carolina. During my rebellion, my relationship with them had been damaged, but the Lord began a process of healing and restoration. I was so broken. The only thing I had to show for my 26 years on Earth was a shattered life.

Although this was the most difficult period in my life, it is a time that I never want to forget. I had to face all of the brokenness and pain that

I had been running from—and confront it sober. However, it was also the first time in my life that I faced my problems with Jesus.

My heart broke as I read God's Word and finally understood what the cross was about. I understood that God loved me so much that He sent His sinless Son to take my punishment. God's love poured into my heart as I begged for His forgiveness and mercy. The Lord gave me four years with my mom before taking her home in April 2000 after a battle with breast cancer. Eight months later, my little brother, Paul, killed himself. The days following their deaths took me down a very difficult road, but the Lord faithfully and gently carried me through.

One day, while visiting my grandmother in Florida, the Lord awakened me in the middle of the night. I had a very strong impression that I was to move to Florida. So the next morning, I told my grandmother that I would be moving down to live with her. She was a recent widow, but she forbade me to come. She didn't want me to give up my life to live with a bunch of old people. I left crying, because I really felt that the Lord had told me to move. However, I soon forgot about it.

Then in April 2003, I quit my job of seven years. On that same day, my grandmother invited me to move in with her in Florida. I prayed to be sure it was truly the Lord's leading, and He confirmed that it was through 1 Timothy 5:16: "If any woman who is a believer has widows in her family, she should help them and not let the church be burdened with them, so that the church can help those widows who are really in need."

So I moved in with my grandmother and began attending Calvary Chapel St. Petersburg. I had already attended two Calvary Chapels while living in South Carolina, so I naturally felt led to try the Calvary Chapel in my new hometown. I soon began looking for ways to get involved. At first, every ministry I tried was a closed door. One Sunday, I prayed with Wendy Hodges, our pastor's wife, about where to get involved. She told me about the **Salt & Light** groups, a ministry that encourages believers to read through the entire Bible at their own pace and then meets together weekly to share insights and memory verses. The Lord had impressed on me that my first ministry was with my grandmother, so I wasn't able to get involved in the **Salt & Light** groups right away.

Sometime around June 2004, I was taking a walk when the Holy Spirit spoke to my heart "salt and light." So I started attending a meeting at Debbie Friley's house. Debbie is responsible for pioneering the **Salt & Light** ministry at Calvary Chapel. I attended her group for a while, and then she began encouraging me to facilitate a group of my own. At first I hesitated, but about a year later, Pastor Danny said in one of his messages, "You need to take that step of faith in leadership, even if you don't feel certain that the Lord is leading you."

At the end of the service, I asked a prayer counselor to pray with me regarding this matter. That same day, I spoke with my **Salt & Light** group leader. Our group had grown and gone out on our own by then, so the leader was no longer Debbie Friley. My new leader confirmed God's message to me by speaking the same words as Pastor Danny! I knew the Lord wanted me to step out in faith. Before long, God worked out the details, and I began leading a group.

Since my conversion, the Bible has been and always will be a book that I read daily. Being in **Salt & Light** has given me the opportunity to share God's Word with others and to hear what others are receiving through His Word. I have also gained new sisters whom I never would have met had it not been for this precious ministry.

Right now, I am very excited about an opportunity the Lord has presented to me. About seven years ago, long before attending Calvary Chapel St. Petersburg and the **Salt & Light** group, I heard the Holy Spirit speak to me in prayer one day. He said, "Budapest." At the time, I thought it was for one of the girls in my teen Bible study who was getting ready to go on a mission trip to Romania. When I called her and told her what I had heard the Lord say, she said, "We are going to Bucharest, but maybe we will go to Budapest." I never thought another thing about it until years later when I met a lady named Elizabeth Jacquier in my **Salt & Light** group. One day, she asked me if I would like to go with her on a trip to Budapest. I suddenly knew that I was supposed to go. I also finally understood why I had heard "Budapest" all those years ago!

Elizabeth and I immediately began praying for our trip. In the meantime, I had the opportunity to go with a group from our church to minister at **New Beginnings**, a nine-month program in Central Florida for teen girls dealing with addiction. After sharing my testimony with the group, we began the long ride home. I told the other ladies in the group about my plans to go to Budapest and that I would be sharing my testimony there.

One of the ladies asked if it was a mission trip. I told her, "Yes, but there are only two of us going." She said, "Do you have the money you need?" I just looked at her, stunned. I couldn't say a word, because we didn't have all the money. In fact, Elizabeth and I had just prayed about the money two days earlier. When I didn't respond, the woman said, "Whatever you need, you've got it!" I was so blown away by her generosity. Needless to say, we were both in tears after that!

Since that time, God has even provided free round-trip airfare for us. Praise the Lord! I believe that God has a special plan for this trip and that we are going to reap a harvest. God wants people saved, and we want His will to be done!

The Lord has used the ministry of Calvary Chapel St. Petersburg in so many ways in my life. Along with the great teaching that I receive, I have also been given opportunities to publicly share my testimony and use my spiritual gifts. The Lord has used many friendships here at Calvary to impact my life. He has used Debbie Friley, one of His great cheerleaders, to encourage me to be steadfast. In addition to facilitating a **Salt & Light** group, I am also a prayer counselor now, which is a dream come true. I feel as though I've been given a great gift to be trusted in a spiritual position. Being accepted as a new creation has enabled me to blossom!

I also go into the Juvenile Detention Center once a month with Calvary Chapel's **JDC Ministry**. Karen Errico, a friend and member of the JDC team, has been very influential in my life in regard to this ministry. Her love for the girls at JDC is so evident and contagious. It has been so awesome to see the girls come to Jesus and to be a part of what the Lord is doing! I have learned so much and been so blessed by the girls that I go to "minister" to.

At this writing, it has been 10 years since I came to the cross of Jesus Christ. So many changes have happened in my life. I am not angry at the world anymore or bound in hatred and unforgiveness. When I met Jesus and experienced His love for me, I knew that He expected me to forgive everyone who had hurt me. With His help, I have forgiven each one. Now I am totally set free from the darkness and live in the light of His love.

Brooke Donnelly, 1994

Brooke Donnelly today, 2007

Chapter 16

Let Man Not Separate

DAVID AND MARIANNE MARCUM
By Mary Fairchild

For this reason a man will leave his father and mother and be united to his wife, and the two will become one flesh. So they are no longer two, but one. Therefore what God has joined together, let man not separate.

—Mark 10:7–9

Dave and Marianne met in 1985 at a church meeting. They quickly fell in love and married in July of 1986. Literally and figuratively, their paths had brought them together from worlds apart.

Dave was born in Columbus, Ohio. His father was an alcoholic, and his mother tried very hard to keep the family together. In spite of her efforts, the state authorities ended up removing the children from the home while Dave was still very young. Eventually his oldest sister, who was married, gained custody of Dave, and they moved to Florida when he was not quite five years old. Years later, Dave's parents also moved to Florida and took up residence in the house next door.

Dave spent his childhood in Pinellas Park, Florida. Although his mother and sister were both Christians, their influence made little impression on him as a youth. "I got involved in local sports, mainly baseball at Davis Field," he recalls. "When I reached my teens, I had a good friend named Arnie. We did everything together. The beginning of my drug use started around age 12 or 13. By the time I got into high school, I started drinking a lot."

Dave went from being an honor roll student in ninth grade to quitting school in the last semester of his tenth grade year. "I squeaked by with my GED," he says. After quitting school, Dave worked different jobs, although he admits that "one lasted a week, one lasted a day, and one I was involved with robbing . . . By the time I was 17, I was heavily into drugs and drinking, fighting, having blackouts, and having car wrecks all the time."

At age 18, Dave landed his first DUI charge. "That was when the state started the driving schools and abuse evaluation programs," he says. "I had to go through it to get my license back. I did, and the program worked for a little while. But then I started drinking again, only worse."

When Dave was 20, he had a remarkable experience while watching an evangelist on television. He recalls, "I thought he was talking right to me! My heart was pounding. I was sweating and crying. I got on my knees and asked Jesus into my life." Immediately, Dave experienced dramatic changes in his life. "I didn't hang with my same friends," he says. "I met another believer, and we got involved in a church where I later met my wife, Marianne!"

Marianne was born in the Detroit area. She was the oldest of three children. Her father worked for Chrysler Corporation and was transferred to Bogota, Colombia, when Marianne was nine years old. "We had a great life!" she says, fondly recalling those early years. "My 'Indiana Jones' dad kept our lives full of excitement, and my godly mom kept our family focused on the Lord."

Although her father was not a believer, the strong faith of Marianne's mother made an eternal impact on her life. "I was raised in the church since I was one week old," she says. "My mom would lay me on the pew. I asked Jesus into my life when I was five. Later, when I was

13, one Christmas Eve the pastor at the Baptist church we attended gave an altar call while we were all singing 'O Come All Ye Faithful.'" That night, Marianne consciously made a decision to surrender her life to the Lord. "I remember sobbing for hours," she says. "My mom told me to start reading my Bible every day. I read the book of Mark first."

Marianne credits God and His faithfulness for keeping her from getting into trouble as she grew older. "Even though I didn't always do things 'as unto the Lord' as a teenager, I didn't want to get involved in the things my friends did, because I didn't want to hurt my parents," she says. "Now that I am older and understand more, I translate that to mean not wanting to hurt the Lord."

Growing up in Colombia, Marianne could have easily fallen in with the wrong crowd. "In Colombia, drugs were everywhere," she explains. "One house we lived in had marijuana growing in our inside garden! My parents entertained a lot. My dad drank and always had a bar. All of their parties had alcohol. My mom only drank coffee. I remember being around all those people as a kid, and I would watch as the night went on and their personalities would change. That bothered me."

Peer pressure was not an issue for Marianne. "As I got into high school and we would go to all the parties, at the beginning of the night we would all have fun dancing and listening to music, but then my friends would become different people by the end of the night. They would make fun of me for not trying to smoke or drink—calling me 'goodie two shoes' or 'Jesus freak.' But then they would call and ask me whose house the youth group was at on Sunday night so they could come. Or when they had relationship problems, they would ask me to pray for them."

Marianne's parents made it clear to her that going to college was not optional. "I really had a heart for people," she says. "I wanted to help them. I wanted to work in some social service field, but I didn't want a career. I just knew I wanted to be married." Even so, Marianne left her family in Colombia to attend a Christian college in California. Once there, she struggled to readjust to American culture and living far from home. "I found comfort and release from stress by eating," she says. "Even though I have never had a drink, taken drugs, or smoked cigarettes, I can somehow relate to people with addictions, because I struggle with overeating. I think the basic issue is the same. Although food is not mind altering, it still takes the place of Christ as Lord in our lives."

After her first year of college, Marianne returned home to Colombia to regroup and choose her next step. "I decided to move back to Michigan to finish my degree," she says. "I had all of my relatives there and a good support group and a church. There I became grounded in a church and continued to grow in the Lord."

After graduating college with a degree in sociology, Marianne had difficulty finding a job. She wanted to work in a social service industry, but when her high hopes were dashed, she began to get depressed. "I was working part-time at K-Mart and babysitting. My dad was not pleased. I decided that to get out of my 'depression,' I needed to go backpacking through Europe. My parents agreed to give me a loan and let me go as long as I contacted them every two weeks. So off I went on my journey to find myself."

During her six-week European journey, Marianne experienced awesome, faith-building adventures and met interesting people. She drew closer to the Lord, and her depression lifted. However, when she returned home, she still could not find a job.

At about that time, a friend of her family in South St. Petersburg, Florida, invited her to move to Florida and stay in her house until it sold. "I counseled with my pastor," she says. "He prayed with me, and with a peace in my heart, I put all my stuff in storage and within three days, moved. I contacted a church that I had been referred to. It was Word of Life in Kenneth City. The pastor and his wife happened to live on my same street—Bahama Shores Drive! They picked me up, and from that day on, I got involved. I found a job a week later and really began my life here."

During the next couple of years, Marianne's friends began praying for her future husband. "One day, the women in the church were teasing me about getting married and asking how they could pray," she recalls. "I said, 'Isn't there anyone out there with a heart after God like King David?' After that, they would pray for my 'David.' I never knew his name would actually be David!"

Marianne and Dave's first meeting was on a Wednesday night. "Dave was with a friend in the fellowship hall," she explains. "I went over and introduced myself. Dave was funny and easy to talk to, and I liked laughing with him." Although they came from vastly different worlds, their lives had intersected in Kenneth City, Florida. God had brought them together, and soon they would join in marriage as one flesh. Marianne says, "I knew that if Dave had not gotten saved, our paths would not have even crossed. He had been involved in every kind of thing I had not. But I also knew that God was all powerful and that He makes all things new."

Marianne and Dave's early years of marriage were blessed with happiness. "We had a trusting relationship, and really, it was very easy," Marianne says. "We never had any in-law problems, and we did everything together. We were the 'DINKS'—double income, no kids. We never planned ahead, just kind of lived day by day. We worked as youth leaders and enjoyed our friends."

> "I knew that if Dave had not gotten saved, our paths would not have even crossed. He had been involved in every kind of thing I had not."

As Dave and Marianne continued to serve in their local church ministry, they experienced a series of intense disappointments. Their hearts went through devastation after devastation as they watched their spiritual leaders fall into sin and their church families torn apart. They bounced from church to church for a while, looking for a firmer foundation where they could become planted. They sought a solid, Bible-teaching church.

One day, in March 1997, their friend Ross White, who was also looking for a church to call home, invited Dave and Marianne to try visiting Calvary Chapel with him. Instantly, they all felt at home. Dave was a drummer, and though the church service was very different than anything he had ever experienced before, he was captivated when the senior pastor turned out to be the drummer in the church worship band. From that day on, Dave and Marianne let their roots sink deep as they got plugged in and became an active part of the family at Calvary Chapel.

Dark days, however, waited on the horizon for Dave and Marianne. Dave remembers, "As the years went on, we became more involved in church, but I drifted farther and farther away from my responsibilities as a husband, as a Christian, and as a father. I never fully surrendered my addictions and began abusing prescription drugs, not only from doctors but also from friends."

By this time, Dave and Marianne had two boys, and Marianne was busy being a mother and working a job. She never suspected that her King David was losing the battle—the war in his soul. "I started noticing that he would take money out of the bank more frequently," she says. "One day, a fear came over me that he was spending it on something he shouldn't be. I was not good at confrontation, but I managed to ask him about it. Very defensively, he told me to mind my own business."

The pressures of life continued to intensify. Dave's parents were both battling cancer, and within a two-month time frame, both Dave and Marianne suffered great losses. After taking a trip to North Carolina for a combination family reunion and Christmas vacation, Marianne recalls, "Christmas morning, we awoke and Dave said he had a dream that his mom had died. That was around 8 A.M. After everyone opened their presents, the phone rang around 11 o'clock. It was Dave's brother, saying that his mom had died that morning around 8 A.M.

"Then two months later, my mom got a fever that lasted for weeks. They ran all kinds of tests on her and determined that the pain in her stomach was her gall bladder. When they opened her up, they found she was full of cancer. She never did get out of the hospital, and she died two weeks later of pancreatic cancer. The grief was severe, and now we were each left without our moms, whom we were both very close to."

Marianne dealt with her grief by staying busy with life. Dave returned to drinking. When he finally admitted to Marianne his struggle with addiction, she was devastated. "I despised him," she says. "I had neither respect nor trust for him. As he continued his lifestyle, I became more and more bitter and slipped further away from him." Dave went downhill quickly. Although Marianne sought assistance, he pushed away everyone who tried to help.

The cracks of separation began to widen. "We did everything apart," Marianne says. "The boys and I even traveled without him. He was content just watching his TV and being alone. Because I did my own thing, I had no idea how bad he was. Then in 2004, I'd had enough. Things kept getting worse, he was very harsh, and I no longer could hide it from the children. Dave was spiraling downward fast, and I was freaking out. I didn't know what to do."

Marianne was also fearful of Dave's anger and violence. At this crucial point, Kirk and Sue Hoatson, two of Marianne and Dave's friends, intervened into the situation. Dave and Marianne had originally made a connection with the Hoatsons through their ministry together in one of the Calvary Chapel children's ministry bands. Over time, the two couples had formed a bond. After working through similar trials of their own, God had prepared Kirk and Sue to assist during the most difficult period of Dave and Marianne's marriage.

All four of them met together one night. They convinced Dave that he needed to move out of the house so that Marianne and the children could be safe and so that he could seek help. Dave moved out the next day and checked into a hotel. He was close to reaching a turning point, but Marianne had reached the breaking point. She wanted a divorce from Dave and came very close to getting it. In fact, the divorce papers were written and ready to be filed. She remembers, "During this time I was feeling abandoned, disillusioned, and unloved. My dreams of marriage were shattered. Forgiveness soon turned to unforgiveness and bitterness, and the roots went deep. My heart was hard."

Meanwhile, Dave began to seek help. "I was destroying my marriage, my wife, my children, and my life!" he says. "Another DUI, another program . . . none of it would shake me . . . until my wife wrote up papers of divorce. I did not want to face reality and my failure." Dave was presented with a series of options, but every door seemed to slam shut. He talked to **Calvary House** in Fort Lauderdale, Teen Challenge, and Taking It to the Streets. Still, the doors would not open.

Although Dave didn't know it, God was working His plan and leading him right to **Calvary House** in St. Petersburg, a brand new ministry of Calvary Chapel St. Petersburg. Dave was about to become the very first man to enter the discipleship program of this pioneering Christian recovery house for men struggling with addictions. At the time, Bob D'Amico was working with Pastor Danny to prepare to open the doors to **Calvary House**. Bob was also in daily communication with Dave, evaluating him for the program. "Bob would not give up on me," Dave recalls. "He put me through some things to see how serious I was about getting sober, but he would not give up on me."

In September 2004, Dave was literally at the end of all hope when he was finally accepted into the **Calvary House** program. "There, I got one on one with Jesus," Dave says. "I opened up my Bible, something I hadn't done in years. I got a daily plan and started reading. Every morning we had devotions. It lit me up. The Word was just washing me. I got one on one in prayer, spending time with Him. There weren't a lot of guys in the house at the time, so I got on my knees a lot. At my worst times, missing my family, missing the boys, I discovered what I was really missing the most was God."

> "At my worst times, missing my family, missing the boys, I discovered what I was really missing the most was God."

One day, while reading in Psalms, Dave couldn't help but recall with longing his many years of leading praise in church worship bands. Psalm 42:4 came to life as he read, "These things I remember as I pour out my soul: how I used to go with the multitude, leading the procession to the house of God, with shouts of joy and thanksgiving among the festive throng." Through intimate times like these with God, Dave says, "Something just broke in me. The obsession started to leave. I started to fill my mind with the good things of God. His Word was washing me, renewing my mind. My time at **Calvary House** was a sanctuary."

While Dave was in the **Calvary House** program, Marianne experienced a sense of peace for the first time in years. She still struggled, however, with embracing the hope that Dave would truly change. She had lost faith and trust in him, and so she decided to remain firm in her resolve to proceed with the divorce. After Dave had been in the **Calvary House** program for more than eight months, Pastor Danny, his wife, Wendy, and Bob D'Amico met with Marianne and urged her to reconsider her plans for divorce. They could see the changes in Dave and believed that God still had a beautiful plan for uniting Dave and Marianne together in marriage.

Marianne's defenses were still very high at the time, and she resisted their counsel. But with the anger she now felt toward her pastor and the church leadership, she knew that she could not continue to serve the Lord with these attitudes in her heart. She began to earnestly seek the Lord, and as a result, He slowly tore down her defensive walls.

A couple of months later, Marianne decided to attend the Passionate Pursuit Women's Conference, where Anne Graham Lotz was ministering. She went to the conference knowing that it was time for her to make a definitive decision about the divorce. With her female companions from Calvary Chapel as witnesses, Marianne specifically asked God for a "neon sign" as to whether or not she should go through with the divorce. From the moment she entered into worship, God began exposing and pulling down the barriers around her heart. She spent a great deal of time that weekend in honest evaluation and in genuine repentance.

On the last morning of the conference, God indeed held up a neon sign for Marianne when Jill Briscoe rose to speak and asked everyone to turn to 1 Corinthians 7. Marianne says, "She went right to verse 27, and here's what she said in her English accent: 'In light of this present situation, if you are married, do not seek a divorce.' Off she went, and that was it! It shined so bright. Here was my sign! I could see it as clear as day."

That morning, Marianne surrendered her marriage, her plans for divorce, and her entire life to the Lord. She prayed, "Lord, Dave doesn't deserve it, but I'm going to do it for You." From that moment forward, Marianne's heart toward Dave began to undergo a transformation. She says, "I'm learning as I look back that once you take a step of obedience, it doesn't mean you know where you're going. It doesn't mean anything else, it just means once you've taken the step, the Lord starts changing things. My heart was softening. I could see things clearer."

In September 2005, Dave became the first official graduate of the **Calvary House** program in St. Petersburg. Marianne remembers the changes she saw in Dave. "He came over, and I could tell his speech was different. He was genuine about his walk with the Lord and serious about now being a father and a husband."

God continued the restoration process between Dave and Marianne, rejoining what had been torn apart. In November 2005, on Thanksgiving weekend, Dave moved back home and was reunited with his family. "If it weren't for the resurrection power of Jesus Christ," he says, "we'd be one more statistic of divorce. He restored my relationship with my kids. He restored my life and my relationship with Him!"

With renewed hope, Marianne says, "Now we are walking with the Lord daily. Tomorrow is not promised to us, but if it comes, we know we will walk with Jesus together through the circumstances until the day we see Him face to face."

Currently, Dave continues to work with the men enrolled in the **Calvary House** program. "I tell the guys now, you've got to want Christ more than anything else," he says. "You've got to want Him more than you want to be free from drugs. You've got to want Him more than you want your wife and more than you want your children." Marianne also ministers one on one with women facing similar experiences of brokenness and bitterness in marriage.

In July 2006, Dave and Marianne celebrated their twentieth wedding anniversary. They are no longer two but truly one flesh. Their experiences have taught them to be much more open and honest with each other. In return, they have a deeper understanding and appreciation for one another. Although their journey as husband and wife threatened to return them once again to separate worlds, it has now brought them closer to each other and nearer to the Lord. They are committed to glorifying God together as one, for as long as they both shall live.

David and Marianne Marcum

Chapter 17

My Weed-Free Life

DOUG LARDNER

For God, who said, "Let light shine out of darkness,"
made His light shine in our hearts to give us the light
of the knowledge of the glory of God in the face of
Christ.

—2 Corinthians 4:6

I was working one day, spraying bugs, when my customer said, "Have you ever visited this Calvary Chapel over here?" He lived in the Mainlands subdivision across the street from the church. "One day I counted over 400 cars." I thought to myself, *He must have a lot of time on his hands.* Then he said, "The Holy Spirit must live there."

And so it began. On January 6, 2002, I visited Calvary Chapel. When I heard Pastor Danny speaking on the armor of God, I knew I was home. I had known the Lord for about three months at the time. I also knew I needed to start separating myself from my sinful past, as Romans 6:6 clearly explains: "For we know that our old self was crucified with him so that the body of sin might be done away with, that we should no longer be slaves to sin."

So I stopped all my old habits, such as smoking cigarettes and weed (marijuana). I threw away my porn videos and quit hanging out with people who did the things I wanted to stay away from. However, because of my pride, just a few months later all of these habits came back again in full force. As Proverbs 11:2 says, "When pride comes, then comes disgrace, but with humility comes wisdom." Now that I was saved, I felt completely disgraced because of my lifestyle. I didn't want to be at Calvary Chapel, where people actually cared and would pray for me. Besides, I was enjoying my sin. So I fell out of fellowship for a short time.

One thing I can say about Calvary Chapel is that the people do pray and care about how your walk with the Lord is going. So whenever someone asked, I made sure they knew what was going on in my life. Bringing light into the darkness was a major part of my recovery. I was not ashamed to tell everyone about the sin in which I was caught. It was only a matter of time before my heart was changed and my desire to serve Christ was back. I wanted to be sold out for my King. So on January 28, 2004, I rededicated my life to God with tears of sorrow. I went to the altar and prayed. I was so sad about how I was living my life that I could not stop crying.

> I told everyone I was a pothead and that I didn't want to be one any longer.

By this time, my bad habits were like huge mountains in my life. In Matthew 17:20, Jesus says, "I tell you the truth, if you have faith as small as a mustard seed, you can say to this mountain, 'Move from here to there' and it will move. Nothing will be impossible for you." This verse weighed heavily on my heart, for I knew that if Jesus said this, it was true. I desperately wanted to have faith that He could move those mountains in my life. So I started reading the Word more than ever. But because I was still smoking weed, every time I would read a passage of Scripture, I would forget what I read.

I must interject here that I had tried to quit smoking weed at least two dozen times. By April 2004, my nicotine habit was under control, thanks to the Lord, but the weed was still a major stronghold. I realized that I needed to start doing things differently, such as reading God's Word first thing in the morning, getting plugged into a small group like Pastor Danny always talked about, and not hanging out with people who drew me away from God.

The very next Sunday, God spoke directly to me through Pastor Danny when he said, "We have to stop hanging out with people who are bringing us down, even those who call themselves Christians." When the altar call came, God led me right to Chris Harris, a prayer counselor and **Life Group** leader. We prayed, and he told me he was having a Bible study at his house the next day. It's so awesome how God works! The next day at the Harris's **Life Group**, I told everyone I was a pothead and that I didn't want to be one any longer.

Getting plugged in was the best move I could have ever made. James 5:16 says, "Therefore confess your sins to each other and pray for each other so that you may be healed. The prayer of a righteous man is powerful and effective." That's exactly what I did. I confessed and Jesus healed me. Chris and Betsy Harris prayed specifically that weed would become nasty to me. I openly admit that the last four times I smoked, it tasted nasty, unlike the thousands of other times that I had smoked before. Praise God!

October 26, 2004 was day number one of my weed-free life. Without prayer, getting plugged in, and getting into God's Word every day, I don't think freedom would have been possible. Thank You, Jesus!

Doug and Brandice met at Calvary Chapel and
were married on August 12, 2006

Chapter 18
Filled With a Mission

Tony and Ellyn Novak
By Ellyn Novak

> For everything that was written in the past was written
> to teach us, so that through endurance and the encour-
> agement of the Scriptures we might have hope.
> —Romans 15:4

After being separated several times, everything was finally going much better for Tony and Ellyn. They were moving ahead with their lives. Ellyn, who had married Tony just three months after her divorce from her husband of 19 years, had seriously wondered whether or not she had done the right thing by remarrying so quickly. But after their third separation, Ellyn knew that she could not live without Tony. The couple didn't know what kept drawing them back to each other, but they were happier now, and their lives seemed to finally be settling down.

A new career was blooming for Ellyn, and Tony's commercial glass business was growing. Many of the material possessions they had always desired had become a reality. Their relationship had taken a turn for the better, and they were now looking forward to sharing a great future together. Yes, everything was going well, except for one thing: there was a great big hole in their hearts that nothing seemed to fill.

Ellyn and Tony were thirsty for something but couldn't put their finger on what it was. Ellyn read several self-help books and even tried yoga. Tony plunged into freshwater fishing and became an avid tournament fisherman. Yet all of the "stuff" they acquired and all the activities they engaged in simply did not fill the hole in their hearts. They started thinking that this was all there was to life: looking toward the goal, reaching it, and then starting with another goal. Life had become boring, and there seemed to be no end to the vicious cycle. No hope.

On the outside Tony and Ellyn appeared to be very happy. But on the inside they were becoming desperate. To make matters worse, they did not speak of their growing despair with each other.

> There was a great big hole in their hearts that nothing seemed to fill.

One day, a fellow glass contractor asked Tony to help him with some extra work. During the first week, Tony came home and told Ellyn that this man was really strange. He was mixing his faith in God with his business, and frankly, it was making Tony a little uncomfortable. In fact, this man kept a Bible on his desk and referred to it often.

Tony's background was Catholic, but he had forgotten most of his religious upbringing due to his drug-filled teenage years. Tony had turned his life around and quit the drugs, but he really didn't want anything to do with religion. He didn't understand some of the things the contractor was talking about, but he listened anyway and later relayed what was said to Ellyn.

Ellyn suggested to Tony that if he was feeling that uncomfortable, he should quit the job and move on. But Tony kept the job and also kept telling Ellyn everything the contractor said. What neither of them knew was that the Lord was working on their hearts—and on that big hole. Because both Tony and Ellyn were too embarrassed to tell each other that a change was happening, they avoided any conversation about the truth of what the contractor was speaking.

Once in a while Tony would pick up an old Bible. Neither of them could remember where they had gotten it, but just before they went to sleep at night, Tony would read some of the things that the contractor had talked to him about and then read them aloud to Ellyn. They would say goodnight, and then both would lay awake mulling over the Word, fearful that something was changing in their hearts and that the other would never understand.

And then it happened. One day while Tony was driving his truck, he heard a speaker on a Christian radio station give an invitation for people to follow Christ. Tony knew that it was time and pulled over to the side of the road. It was there that he gave his life to the Lord. He cried and knew the hole in his heart had just been filled with the Holy Spirit.

A couple of hours later, Ellyn was in her office reading an e-mail from a friend. It was a chain letter that she would usually delete before reading, but this one was about God and His love. She knew that it was time and asked Jesus into her life. She cried and knew that the hole in her heart had been filled.

Neither Ellyn nor Tony called the other. In fact, they both became nervous about how they were going to explain what had happened. Their usual Friday night ritual was to meet at a local restaurant. That night, they each pulled up in the parking lot and prayed that God would give them the words to tell the other what had happened in their lives. When Ellyn walked up to Tony's truck, she told him that she had something very important to tell him. But Tony said he had something to tell her—and it had to be more important than what she had to say. They decided to go inside and talk.

After ordering, Tony went first and told Ellyn he had given his life to the Lord. He waited for her to laugh or give him a blank stare, but instead he saw a big tear running down her face. She told him that she had done the same thing at the office. By now they were both dabbing their eyes and blowing their noses. When the waitress came to the table, she was very sympathetic and asked if someone had died. They responded, "Yes, we did!"

The next day, Ellyn and Tony went out and bought new Bibles. They could not get enough of the Word. They told Tony's contractor friend what had happened, and he was ecstatic. But something was missing. They needed to find a church and be around other Christians. They really needed to learn what to do next.

After a few weeks of discussion, Ellyn and Tony decided they didn't want to attend a Catholic or Lutheran church but find something completely different. One day, Tony was given a job to install a wall of mirrors at a house in St. Petersburg. He was invited inside by the owner and immediately noticed there were no personal items in the house. It seemed void, except for a few pieces of furniture. When Tony asked the owner, Steve, if he had just moved in, he said he had lived there for several years.

Steve then asked Tony what was new in his life, and Tony told him the incredible story of how he and Ellyn had found the Lord. Steve was excited and asked if they had found a church yet. When Tony said no, Steve told him about a small church meeting in a warehouse and how the pastor was the drummer in the band. Steve told Tony he taught in the children's ministry and everyone knew him. Tony said they would try it out.

So the next Sunday, Ellyn and Tony went to Calvary Chapel. At first the service seemed weird to them, as it was held in a warehouse. There was a stage with rock 'n' roll instruments, and everyone was dressed in blue jeans. However, both Ellyn and Tony knew they wanted something different, so they sat and waited for the service to start. Everyone was very friendly, introduced themselves, and shook Tony and Ellyn's hands.

When the music started, Ellyn and Tony found themselves clapping and smiling—something they had never done in their previous churches. The pastor was the drummer, and the message was exactly what they were looking for: truth in its purest form, direct from the Bible.

After the service, Tony and Ellyn got into their car and looked at each other. Ellyn told Tony she really liked it, and he said he really liked it as well. But Tony was concerned. He thought that it was a little rude that people kept trying to ask questions with their hands up during the worship! Ellyn agreed that it seemed a bit strange. Despite this concern, Ellyn and Tony kept going every Sunday, and that hole in their hearts continued to stay filled. Eventually, they realized that the people were praising the Lord, not trying to ask questions. They also started lifting their hands in praise!

Tony and Ellyn wanted to thank Steve for leading them to Calvary, but when they asked about him at church, they were told that there was no Steve in the children's ministry. Tony went back to the contractor who had given him the job at Steve's house to look up the address, but they could not find the invoice on which it was written. Tony went back to the neighborhood to find the house, but all of the houses looked the same, and he could not remember which one it was. They could only wonder about what had happened to Steve. Deep inside, they knew God had been instrumental through it all.

Soon, Ellyn and Tony started going to church on Wednesday nights as well. They drank in every word and started to grow as they were fed through the teaching. Being around other Christians gave them good examples to follow as they matured in their faith. They felt at home, and eventually they also decided to volunteer at the Missions Café, serving coffee and donuts before services.

Three months later, Tony went on his first mission trip. God put a burden for missions in his heart, and after going on a trip together, God put missions in Ellyn's heart, too. Believing that God would someday lead them to the mission field full time, Ellyn left her corporate job to work in the church office as Missions Assistant and Office Manager. Tony continued in short-term missions, completing his twenty-second trip this year.

Currently, God has led the Novaks to the mission field they least expected—their hometown of Erie, Pennsylvania. They are starting a home-based Bible study that they hope, Lord willing, will grow into a Calvary Chapel church plant. Tony has given up his business, and Ellyn has left her position on the church staff to move north and spread the warmth of Christ in a town as spiritually cold as its winter climate.

Thank the Lord that He never gave up on this anxious couple with big holes in their hearts! Praise God for filling their lives with the love, grace, and mercy they now seek to share with other empty hearts in need of the Savior.

Tony and Ellyn Novak

Chapter 19

There is Joy in Pain

PATRICIA HODSON

For our light and momentary troubles are achieving for
us an eternal glory that far outweighs them all.
—2 Corinthians 4:17

During our lesson one Sunday morning, I asked the fourth grade
students, "Can anyone tell me what idolatry is?"

"I can," answered a familiar voice.

"All right, Tommy, go ahead."

With all sincerity he replied, "It's a place where everything costs a
dollar."

This story isn't an e-mail joke, and it didn't come out of a *Reader's
Digest*. It's just one of the many memories I have of teaching Sunday
School at Calvary Chapel.

I had enjoyed teaching Sunday School at Calvary Chapel for five
years. Things in my life were running smoothly. I had a family I adored,
a job I really liked, and I was six classes into fulfilling my dream of

being a teacher. I was blessed with good health. I had even lost weight and was running my first company marathon. Little did I know that my perfect world was about to be shaken, my faith tested, and my priorities turned around.

During a rather routine operation in 1997, a nerve was accidentally damaged that left me with a condition called inguinal neuralgia. The neuralgia caused a severe and chronic pain unlike anything I had ever felt or heard about. It is difficult to explain in words the constant sensation of burning fire under my skin. I cannot escape the pain, even in my sleep. I often wake up from dreams where I cry out in pain. I weep on the ground in these nightmares. When I awake, I soon realize the pain is not just a nightmare but very real.

Being the stubborn person that I am, I tried to just live with the pain for a while. I struggled hard to shake it off and keep working. I didn't want to give up my job. I often used the quote, "If you find a job you love, you'll never have to work a day in your life." Nor did I want to quit going to school. I had finally made it back after many years, my company was paying 100 percent of the tuition, and I had a 4.0 GPA. But the pain soon became debilitating. I had the first of what would be 21 operations to "fix" the problem.

College turned out to be the first thing to go, and when it did, so did my dream of becoming a teacher. It took some intervention from my family, doctors, and colleagues to convince me to leave work and go on disability. I tried for a long time to call it "medical leave," with the intent of getting better and going back, but it was not to be.

My mission in finding pain relief soon turned to an obsession. My journey included acupuncture, chiropractors, physical therapy, laser treatment, radio frequency treatment, cryogenics, neurectomies, three trials for a morphine pump, several trials for a spinal cord stimulator, and many different medications. In all, I had more than 20 surgeries in less than three years and was taking 17 different medications each day. During this time, I also let desperation take over my convictions and did a few things I am not very proud of. I knew these things did not please God, and He quickly showed me that even if they did give me some relief, it was not worth the price of sinning against Him.

I started to long for healing. It was my total focus. I now see that my longing was more like coveting. I would watch the TV evangelists and wait for them to call out my affliction so that I would be healed. I had the faith to touch that TV screen. I also insisted that my husband smash up a cutting board that had horoscope signs on it. It had been built into our kitchen counter long before we moved into the house, but I was convinced that I would be healed once this satanic artifact was out of my house. We look back now and laugh at this, but it was a sad reality as to how far my longing had gone. I wound up with a big hole in my counter and was still in pain.

Desperation became depression. I cried constantly. I had no joy. I had no hope. Because much of my self-worth had been wrapped up in my job and the things I planned and did for my family, I felt completely useless. I went from being unstoppable to being nearly bedridden. Super mom was definitely gone. I traded in my nice fitted business suits for pajamas or anything with elastic.

> I went from being unstoppable to being nearly bedridden. Super mom was definitely gone.

As the perfect planner, my Day Runner calendar had run my life. I had my family's life planned out by the year. I was now planning each day around my pain and how I felt. The depth of my depression was more than I or my family and friends could handle.

I recall one time getting a prayer request for someone dying of cancer and actually having jealous thoughts about this person. I knew that her suffering would end but that mine would not. I could not see myself living with this pain for the rest of my life. How could I go on with pain every second of the day? It consumed me. I am embarrassed to say that I even thought of taking this great gift of life that God has given me. I had no hope and could see no hope in my future.

Although I had left work and school, and my social calendar was now down to doctor appointments, I continued to teach Sunday School. Unfortunately, it was only a few months before I lost sight of what God could do and began focusing on what I could no longer do. I was broken, inadequate, substandard, damaged, and unreliable. I felt that I could no longer give the children what they deserved.

I went to our children's pastor, intending to quit teaching Sunday School. He only asked one question: "Are you physically able to teach?" I told him I could if I had a person backing me up. He was very bold to tell me, "Well, you can't quit then. Whose power are you working under?" After speaking with him, I realized that I needed to rely on God's strength and remember how awesome it is that He uses the broken and inadequate.

With that motivation, I continued to teach. Even in pain, the Lord has shown me how important it is to get out of bed to serve Him. He has given me just enough strength to do this—not enough for a 40 to 60 hour workweek, but enough for a few hours on Sunday and time spent with Him preparing each lesson. There are days that I know I would not get out of bed if I did not teach.

Through much encouragement and prayer, I began to see that I was searching for healing when I should have been looking to the Healer. He was my answer. God had it all for me. He gave me support in His Word and through many people in the church, my Christian counselors, and in my quiet times. As soon as I was truly able to focus on Jesus, I was able to pray the words of Paul in 2 Corinthians 12:8–9: "Three times I pleaded with the Lord to take it away from me. But he said to me, 'My grace is sufficient for you, for my power is made perfect in weakness.' Therefore I will boast all the more gladly about my weaknesses, so that Christ's power may rest on me." Yes, God gave me the peace in knowing that I would suffer in pain and that He would walk with me through it.

God has restored so much in my life. I still have severe pain and am still on very strong medication. The difference is that I now also have much joy. I am very grateful for the people of our church who have been obedient to the Lord. People have brought meals, cleaned my house, and prayed for me without ceasing. It was such an encouragement to receive a stack of get well cards from 15 fourth graders wanting Miss Patricia to get well. I know I am still covered in prayer all the time, and for that I am eternally grateful.

There were so many times that my sisters in the Lord would give me a verse, book, card, or note that would encourage me with the Word of God. One example came from Amy Dayton. She did not know me very well and had moved away to Texas. God put me on her mind and told her to send me a book. She later told me she did not understand why, but she was sure it was from God. I am very thankful for her obedience.

The book, *Rose from Brier* by Amy Carmichael, gave me hope that someone who understood pain could have joy. Miss Carmichael was inspired to write this book when she reflected on the fact that most books attempting to comfort sick people were written by the well and missed the mark. From her own personal experience with severe pain and being bedridden, she was able to minister to those of us who know such pain. In her weakness, God's strength was manifested. Through her words, the Lord changed my perspective and my heart. Her words led me back to God's Word.

I am thankful for having such a supportive family. Many spouses leave in times of crisis, but God gave my husband and my children a great amount of mercy and compassion toward me. My husband has never looked at me with anything but love in his eyes. Even during my most painful moments, he truly looks at me as if he thinks I am the most beautiful woman in the world. My children have missed out on a lot, and I have much guilt about that. I am still working through some of these things. Yet throughout this trial, my family has been at my side, praying for me and ministering to me in so many ways. God is good. I am able to see how much joy they give me. I even have a granddaughter now, and she can make anyone smile!

The prayer I have for myself and anyone else who suffers with pain or chronic illness is 2 Corinthians 4:17–18: "For our light and momentary troubles are achieving for us an eternal glory that far outweighs them all. So we fix our eyes not on what is seen, but on what is unseen. For what is seen is temporary, but what is unseen is eternal." It is difficult to think that our afflictions are "light" in nature or that they can ever achieve for us something as wonderful as eternal glory. But this is what God says. It is a promise we can firmly believe.

I recently received a spinal cord stimulator implant that has made things a bit easier. I still have pain and need to take very strong pain medication. There are still days that I am unable to get out of bed. I get frustrated that I can only give half a day to things that are all-day events. My life is changed. I must rest often and ask for help. I accept my weakness with humility. Still, my outlook has gone from looking at how I can get out of my situation to how God can use me *in* my situation.

In Jeremiah 29:11, God tells us, "'For I know the plans I have for you,' declares the LORD, 'plans to prosper you and not to harm you, plans to give you hope and a future.'" I finally believe this fact. I feel that I can now live with joy in spite of the overwhelming pain. I am looking to the Healer instead of obsessing about the healing. I have a promise that one day I will be pain free and without tears. So when people now see me smile, it is no longer a fake smile in which I am trying to look happy. I have real joy inside that overrides my pain and suffering. Only God could take a painful situation and work something wonderful into it.

Of all the things I had to give up, God has allowed me to keep the desire of my heart here at Calvary Chapel. I have the awesome privilege of teaching every Sunday morning, and I have been doing so now for more than 10 years. It may not be the way I planned to be a teacher, but the Lord has given me the grace and strength to serve with joy, even in the midst of pain. He helps me to take my eyes off of my own trouble and gives me a break from my suffering while I serve. As I let go of the past, God fills the future. He has even allowed me to take a role in children's ministry and coordinate the teacher training. I can still use the skills I learned in my previous job for His service. It took a long time, but I rarely look back at the old job. The Lord has truly given me hope and a future.

I thank the wonderful people at Calvary Chapel for their constant prayers and acts of love. I thank Kevin, Amanda, Jeremy, Aly, and Anthony for being a loving and supportive family. I especially thank Jesus, my Savior, my Healer, and my source of great joy.

Patricia Hodson

Chapter 20

Victory Through the Grave of Defeat

Scott Rodriguez

> But he said to me, "My grace is sufficient for you, for my power is made perfect in weakness." Therefore I will boast all the more gladly about my weaknesses, so that Christ's power may rest on me.
>
> —2 Corinthians 12:9

Late one evening in 1997, after having been incarcerated for two years, I prayed earnestly for a godly wife. I remember being overwhelmed almost immediately with a clear answer from God. I don't know how to explain it, but I knew intuitively that God had a wife already picked out for me and that she would be a missionary. I was overcome with joy and thankfulness but also a bit surprised, because I had never considered getting involved in missions.

Two years later I met Crystal. However, by then I had begun living a life of compromise. Crystal was not looking for a godly person, and unfortunately, I was not either. During our first months together, I told her that God had shown me that my wife was to be a missionary. She later became pregnant, and I proposed. We eventually married, and our life increasingly became more ungodly. By the time our daughter was 18 months old, I was arrested on a felony charge of driving without a license and possession of marijuana, which was a violation of my probation.

It was in jail that God once again got my attention. The fear that I might be returned to prison and lose my wife and daughter was crippling. I remember trying to get the jail's psychiatrist to give me medication that would "put me out of it." He refused.

During the days that followed, God began to speak to me and give me the opportunity to return to Him. I was completely broken and had nowhere to go except to Him. I made the decision to turn away from sin and started praying that God would keep my family together. After 23 days, I was released from jail on bond. I was so thankful. I had been told that I probably would not get a bond on a felony violation of probation.

> It was in jail that God once again got my attention. The fear that I might be returned to prison and lose my wife and daughter was crippling.

I had also been praying that God would lead Crystal and me to a church. I had to go! One year before, we had been invited to a service at Calvary Chapel St. Petersburg on a Sunday night. I remembered that service, and together Crystal and I decided that we would go back the next Sunday. When we arrived, we were told right away that if we wanted our daughter to sit with us, we would have to sit in a room in the back of the auditorium called the "Family Room." It didn't bother me too much, but Crystal did not like the idea at all. During the first 10 minutes of the service, she became angrier and angrier. I was secretly praying that God would speak to her heart.

The pastor began his message, which was about church hopping. After preaching for a few minutes, he stopped and said that he wanted to talk about an element of Calvary Chapel that he knew many people had a problem with: the Family Room! He said that parents with young children who were asked to sit in the Family Room often became dissatisfied with the church. He explained that Satan would do anything to keep people out of a godly church and that this was one way Satan went about the task of robbing people of God's intended church home. As he was speaking, I sensed the awesome presence of the Holy Spirit confirming that I was where I belonged. I looked at my wife and could see a change in her countenance. The anger was gone. God was speaking to her.

From that day on, we were at Calvary Chapel every Sunday and Wednesday. Less than three months later, I began to fellowship with a men's Bible study group and to volunteer for **Men of Arms** outings. My wife and I signed up to serve together during the **Angel Tree** Christmas outreach to children of prisoners. Not only had I been a prisoner from age 20 to almost 25, but also I was the child of a prisoner. My father has been in prison most of my life. I could hardly endure **Angel Tree** without crying. It was at that event that I first worshiped with Barnabas, one of the church's outreach bands.

The times of worship at Calvary Chapel were what really made it feel like home for me. I never experienced worship with dry eyes. As time went by, Crystal and I began growing in the Lord. Our daughter became accustomed to the children's ministry, and the Family Room was no longer an issue for us.

In January 2002, we were praying about my upcoming court hearings. I faced the possibility of going back to prison, but we prayed that God would be merciful. One Sunday, Pastor Larry Gray preached a message titled, "God Wins No Ultimate Victory Except Through the Grave of Apparent Defeat." He cited many examples of this, including how our Lord's ultimate victory came only after He had endured the cross. Although I was heavily affected by this message, I tried to twist it to mean that I had already suffered defeat in my arrest and that now God would give me victory by sparing me from prison. Deep inside, however, I knew that the Spirit was preparing me.

On January 24, 2002, I was sentenced to 12.4 years in prison for my violation, with credit for approximately four and a half years I had already served. I now had a fresh eight years of prison ahead of me. As my wife sobbed, I was taken from her and my daughter and led out of the courtroom. I was destroyed again. I felt I would lose my precious wife and daughter forever. There could be no way our marriage would last.

Inside my head I screamed at God over and over again, *Why did You forsake me?* Everything felt surreal. I began thinking, *Escape. You can't bear this—it's too much!* I sensed God trying to tell me that He had not forsaken me, but I pushed His voice away. Ultimately, I did attempt to get away from an officer. I was quickly apprehended and charged with attempted escape. Now I faced an additional 15 years of prison time. I was medicated, stripped of my clothes, and placed in an observation cell on suicide watch. But God was there, and I knew it.

After three days, I went off the medication and surrendered to reality and to God's comfort. I accepted the fact that I was going away to prison and that I couldn't do anything about it. As I sat brokenhearted, my wife, family, and friends at Calvary Chapel began to pray. Everything looked terrible, but we held on to our God. Crystal had to quit college to pay the bills. She needed a job, and God graciously opened the door of employment for her at Calvary Chapel. Working at the church helped her become rooted in the Lord in preparation for a difficult time.

The next two and a half years were hard, but God was with us. I was serving Him inside prison, and Crystal was serving Him outside. She was privileged during this time to go on two short-term mission trips. Many times the church helped us, and various brothers and sisters ministered to my family's countless needs. The **Men of Arms** ministry that I had volunteered with worked on our home several times while I was in prison. They even did the same type of digging for a sewer line that I had earlier done at someone else's home with **Men of Arms**. In addition, my daughter was now on the receiving end of the **Angel Tree** program. God was providing.

While in prison, I began studying Law. I eventually discovered that I had been given an erroneous sentence. In late 2004, I appeared before the court for resentencing. In addition to my family's presence, the courtroom was filled with supportive faces from Calvary Chapel. The error in my sentencing entitled me to a mere reduction of 30 days, but the state agreed to take off 18 months!

Throughout the next year, God continued to bless my family and me. My wife was given two vehicles. We later gave one of them away, and after a few months, it was given back to us with new tires. God provided for my daughter's preschool fees and countless other needs that were faithfully met through the Lord's body. I was also accruing time off for good conduct, and with another small reduction to the sentence, my release was quickly approaching.

As my time in prison winded down, I began praying about two particular issues. First, I prayed for my dad, who was also nearing release from prison. I prayed that he would encounter God through the ministry of Barnabas at his prison, Hardee Correctional Facility. But he wasn't attending the services. I prayed for God to send someone special to minister to him and to show him the love of Christ. For the first time in my adult life, it appeared that my dad and I would be free at the same time. I desperately wanted him to make a successful re-entry into society. Second, I started to pray about my own transition to freedom. I knew it probably wasn't going to be easy and that I would need a lot of grace.

> . . . even my dog remembered me! I had reason to praise God!

On February 13, 2006, I was released from Polk Correctional Institution and joyously reunited with my wife and daughter. My marriage had been in jeopardy, but God had redeemed it. He also granted my desperate desire to continue building a relationship with my daughter. Our home, which had once been in deep foreclosure proceedings, was still ours. And though it may sound kind of silly, even my dog remembered me! I had reason to praise God!

Three weeks later, I was offered a job at Calvary Chapel. I gratefully accepted. After serving for just a short time at Calvary Chapel, I was blessed with many opportunities to share about God's faithfulness to me while I was in prison. Sometimes challenging situations have arisen. For instance, a few times the volunteers I have worked with have asked, "So, when did you first start coming to Calvary?" Knowing that such questions would be asked by those unaware of my recent past, I had determined to always be forthright. "Oh, I found Calvary back in 2001,"

I would reply. To this they would usually say, "Really? Why have I not seen you before?" And I would honestly reply, "Because I just got out of prison a few weeks ago." I must admit that I found some humor in their unsure reactions. I was also surprised once when a man said in return, "Yeah, me too!"

All in all, God's people at Calvary Chapel have been very gracious. The Lord has made me feel like I've come home.

My dad and I did get to share a meal together, but unfortunately he was rearrested. That special person I prayed for still has not been sent, but perhaps my dad is not yet ready to hear. However, I've also learned when I pray for God to send someone, sometimes He says, "Okay, you go." So I've now been blessed to bring God's truth to my dad as he sits again in a jail cell. I've also been able to visit two other men in jail, both of whom I knew while I was incarcerated.

God has given me a heart for His prisoners. I am amazed how quickly the doors of opportunity are opening! Recently, I was asked and approved by my overseers at Calvary to begin going into two local corrections facilities. It was an awesome blessing to be on the receiving end of Calvary's outreach to the incarcerated and needy, but I have no words to justly describe the joy and sense of God's pleasure I felt at being included among those called to reach the all too often forgotten ones. I can only say, "Praise the Lord!"

At Polk Correctional, where I spent my last days as a prisoner, Barnabas, the band I first saw at **Angel Tree**, came every month and brought an atmosphere of worship. It made me feel as if I were at home in Calvary Chapel. Now, as I ponder this, I remember something my pastor once said: "God has a way of making each of us feel as if we're His favorite." I know that Barnabas's prison ministry was special for each inmate, but sometimes I couldn't help but feel that God had sent the group just for me. This is also how I have felt about our church since the first day in the Family Room—that Calvary Chapel was there just for me.

Looking back, I see clearly that God did not forsake me as I had accused Him of doing. No, He brought about an awesome victory through the grave of apparent defeat.

Scott Rodriguez and his wife, Crystal

Glossary

Alpha, "A Beginning," Inc. This ministry meets at a local transitional housing facility and offers supportive services and encouragement to women and teens in crisis pregnancies.

Angel Tree Ministry. Angel Tree is a ministry of Prison Fellowship that delivers love in the form of Christmas gifts and a message of hope to children of prisoners. Calvary Chapel sponsors an Angel Tree Christmas party each year for children of prisoners as well as their caretakers and family. The goal is to connect the parents in prison with their children through church volunteers who deliver Christmas gifts and the message of the gospel.

Calvary House. Calvary House is a residential discipleship ministry for Christian men who are dealing with life-controlling struggles such as drug and alcohol addictions.

JDC Ministry. The Juvenile Detention Center ministry reaches out to teens aged 10 to 17 with the gospel, prayer, teaching, and encouragement. Volunteers meet at the county detention center on Friday nights.

Life Groups. A Life Group is simply a home fellowship. Through the sharing of our lives with one another, Life Groups are designed to encourage and nourish the spiritual life of the members of the church body. Our Life Groups are informal, small groups that meet throughout the week in various homes for a special time of fellowship, prayer, encouragement, and Bible study.

Men of Arms. Men of Arms is a part of our men's ministry that allows men to participate in shared ministry experiences while reaching out to help with home repairs for needy families. The men meet once a month on a Saturday for breakfast at the church and then head out in groups to various job sites.

Men's Accountability Groups. The vision of the men's accountability ministry is to encourage and equip men to courageously assume their God-given responsibility to be leaders in their homes, churches, communities, and in the world. Through prayer, fellowship, sharing of a meal, teaching, honest communication, and shared ministry experiences, the men are challenged to fulfill their male role as defined by the Word of God.

Most Excellent Way. The Most Excellent Way is a ministry designed to help people become free from addictive, compulsive, and life-controlling behaviors. Support is offered to both the addict and the family members.

New Beginnings. New Beginnings is a mentoring outreach to female offenders aged 14 to 17 in a community-based residential facility located in Wauchula, Florida.

Salt & Light. Salt & Light is a growing ministry of small groups developed by Debbie Friley, a member of Calvary Chapel. Believers meet together on a weekly basis to read through the Bible at their own pace, memorize Scripture, and encourage one another in their walk with the Lord.

Women of Heart. Women of Heart is a women's ministry that serves families or people in need of practical help. The volunteer force provides meals, does light housework, and runs errands for members of the church body during times of medical crisis, when a death in the family has occurred, or any time a practical need is presented.